WAKE UP THE WINNER INSIDE

13 Mental Aerobics To Break Down Your Personal Barriers To Success

KARLA BRANDAU

LIFE POWER PUBLISHERS
ATLANTA, GEORGIA

WAKE UP THE WINNER INSIDE

13 Mental Aerobics To Break Down
Your Personal Barriers To Success

 For information, please contact: Life Power Publishers, 4985 Chartley Circle, Lilburn, Georgia 30047, USA. First printing 1999. Designed by John Scriven. Printed and bound in the USA.

10 9 8 7 6 5 4 3 2 1

Although the author and publisher have made every effort to ensure the accuracy and completeness of information contained in this book, we assume no responsibility for errors, inaccuracies, omissions, or inconsistencies herein. Any slights of people, places, or organizations are unintentional.

Brandau, Karla
WAKE UP THE WINNER INSIDE
13 Mental Aerobics To Break Down Your Perosnal Barriers To Success
ISBN No. 1-892908-02-9

For information on keynote speeches and workshops, contact:
Karla Brandau, 4985 Chartley Circle, Lilburn, Georgia 30047, USA. Tel: 770-923-0883 Fax: 770-931-2530
E-mail: karla@kbrandau.com
Website: www.kbrandau.com

Dedication

To Steve,
my best friend and mentor,
for loving me so unselfishly.

Acknowledgments

I'm proud to thank the people whose contributions have helped me to bring this labor of love to fruition.

To my dear family: Susan, my daughter; Chad, my son-in-law; Kenny and Mark, my sons. We have grown up together and experienced the richness of life. Without the lessons we shared, the pages of this book would be blank and my life infinitely empty.

To John Scriven, patient and precise, for his invaluable work of editing and layout.

To Patti Wood and Jean Houston Shore for reading the manuscript and giving insights into subtle changes that made concepts clearer and more readable.

To Vicki Barnes, who has just published *The Kid Book,* for reading the manuscript and offering hours of telephone consulting.

To Margaret Estes for her delightful artwork.

To Richard Weylman who, when I wondered if I could finish this book, reminded me of my own words: Expect Miracles.

To Matt Geary for his ideas in the original conception of the book and for his cover design.

To Hyrum Smith and Dick Winwood who introduced me to the world of speaking 16 years ago.

And finally, to all the winners out there who are in the process of waking up. I hope this book helps.

CONTENTS

THE WARM UP 9

Aerobic One: THE TIGER PRINCIPLE 13

Aerobic Two: THE SWINGING ROPE BRIDGE 25

Aerobic Three: BREATHE IN, BREATHE OUT 35

Aerobic Four: THE BEAUTY MAKE-OVER 45

Aerobic Five: THE LIGHT BULB 55

Aerobic Six: WORKING IN THE ZONE 61

Aerobic Seven: MERLIN AND ROSIE 69

Aerobic Eight: HANDS ON THE OUTSIDE 79

Aerobic Nine: DANDELIONS 87

Aerobic Ten: OPPORTUNITY? 95

Aerobic Eleven: THE WORDS OF WINNERS 105

Aerobic Twelve: THE AIR DYNE BICYCLE 113

Aerobic Thirteen: SEA DEBRIS OR BLUE SKIES? 123

THE COOL DOWN 133

Whoever you are, you can wake up the winner inside every morning of your life.

THE WARM UP

My Minister Stood Up One Cold January Morning and said, "I hope all of you have a lot of problems this year because, if you don't, you'll be dead and we'll miss you greatly. It is problems that challenge you and keep you going."

I thought to myself, "I've got enough problems to last twelve months. I'll still be here at the end of the year." Two or three days later, I came upon this quote by Henry David Thoreau:

"If the day and the night are such that you greet them with joy and life emits a fragrance like flowers and sweet-scented herbs, that is your success."

My mind was filled with the thought that to triumph over life's problems and challenges and wake up every morning with the winner's attitude is the ultimate key to success. I wanted that success, but I wondered where I would find it. After all, I had been "out there" for years searching for it. Then I realized that, before I could wake up in the morning as a winner, I first had to wake up the winner inside.

As I was contemplating how to do this, another powerful thought occurred to me: I did exercises for the body every day, so why not also do exercises for the mind and call them mental aerobics?

Next, my mind went back to junior high school when I learned about our founding fathers. Benjamin Franklin was the founding father who impressed me most, having signed the Constitution, invented bifocals and the Franklin Stove, and discovered electricity.

As if this list were not enough, Franklin also discovered the way to self-improvement. He chose thirteen values and wrote them down in a little black book that he always carried with him. He worked on one value each week. When he had completed all thirteen, he started over. In one year, he went through all thirteen values four times. Through this process he became the man we still study today.

This book was conceived when the idea of mental aerobics and Benjamin Franklin's personal improvement process converged in my mind.

On these pages you will find thirteen mental aerobics. Practice one each week and, in only one year, you'll triumph over the problems that seem overwhelming today. In addition, you'll have built your character and will be on your way to becoming the person of your dreams.

So that you'll be able to get the most from this book, let me familiarize you with the sections. Each chapter contains an explanation of the principles that constitute the aerobic, followed by "Karla's Coaching Corner." In the coaching corner, I give you my insight into how powerful the aerobic can become in your life if you internalize and implement the principles.

Next, because you do conditioning exercises when getting ready to play a competitive sport, I've included a section called "Conditioning Exercises" to help you build mental toughness.

Finally, in a section entitled "When The Winner Awakes," I share ideas about the kinds of decisions and the kinds of changes in behavior you can expect in yourself as you grow mentally and emotionally. These changes will indicate that the winner inside you is waking up. I challenge you to become a different and a better person than you are today by doing the things that will wake up the winner inside you.

Suggestions For Getting The Most Out Of The Book

- Read this book several times.
- Work on one principle each week.
- Make specific goals for enhanced mental attitudes and improved behaviors.

Then you can expect success every day of your life, for there will be no other option.

"When we were on the Ferris wheel, she wanted to be on the rollercoaster."

AEROBIC ONE **1**

THE TIGER PRINCIPLE

DAILY
MENTAL AEROBIC

Today I will live in the present.

"Life is not a dress rehearsal."

ALEXANDRA STODDARD

THE IDAHO STATE FAIR WAS ALWAYS THE EVENT OF THE YEAR, with all the lights, sights and sounds that make kids think they're in wonderland. When Mom and Dad packed us into the car for the trip from New Plymouth to Boise, we knew that Heaven was not far away.

I can still recall those wondrous sights and sounds, along with the delicious taste of cotton candy. But my most vivid memory is of my sister. When we were on the Ferris wheel, she wanted to be on the rollercoaster. When we were on the rollercoaster, she whined to be in the fun house. She could never enjoy the moment. I don't know what it did to her on the inside, but it irritated me on the outside.

As an adult, you may exhibit similar behavior. When you're at home, you think about work, and when you're at work, you think about home. When you're playing tennis, you have this gnawing feeling that you should be cleaning the garage. When you're cleaning the garage, you wish you had time to relax and play tennis.

When you become preoccupied with a time and place that's not in the present, you don't give full attention to the activity of the moment. This reduces productivity and causes you to live in a chaotic mental and emotional state, because you live out of balance.

An ancient fable tells of a man who was being chased by a tiger. As the man was making his escape, he ran off the edge of a cliff. On the way down, he grabbed a branch of a tree that was growing out of the rock. As he looked back up into the gaping jaws of the tiger, he winced at the sight of the claws pawing for him.

He then heard another thunderous roar and looked down. On a ledge just beneath him was another tiger, looking up at him with hungry eyes. Suddenly his life passed before his eyes and disappeared.

As he took a long, deep breath and tried to steady himself, he noticed a wild strawberry growing from the rock. It had been kissed by the sun until it was brilliant red and perfectly ripe. He reached over with one hand and picked the strawberry. Then he ate it and enjoyed it, without worrying about the tigers that were above and below him.

Apply the Tiger Principle in your life. Don't worry about the tigers of the past or the tigers of the future. They will always be there. Approach each moment and live in it as if it were the most precious moment of your life. When you do, you'll find balance and inner peace.

Apply the Tiger Principle in your life.

Karla's Coaching Corner

Guilt and worry, the tigers of the past and the future, are the two most futile emotions you'll ever experience. Both these debilitating emotions keep you upset and prevent you from living in the moment.

Guilt immobilizes you and uses up the precious present by focusing you on past behaviors or events you can't change.

Worry paralyzes you because you're preoccupied with events that *might* happen in the future.

Mark Twain, the great humorist, emphasized the point about worry when he said, "I have experienced many horrible things in my lifetime, a few of which actually happened."

Robert Jones Burette summarized in *Golden Day* how guilt and worry affect behavior:

"It isn't the experience of today that drives men mad. It is the remorse for something that happened yesterday and the dread of what tomorrow may disclose."

Dr. Wayne Dyer, in his book, *Your Erroneous Zones*, states: "If you believe that feeling bad or worrying long enough will change a past or future event, then you're residing on another planet with a different reality system."

He recommends that if you want to take advantage of the NOW and make the most of the present moment in productivity or activities that lead to quality of life, you must get rid of guilt and worry.

As you work on ridding your life of guilt and worry, two courses of action are necessary:

1. It's important to be able to look at past events and learn from small indiscretions, then vow to avoid making the same mistakes again.

This isn't the same as feeling guilty. Guilt is a preoccupation that can run from mild upset to severe depression. Learning from your mistakes is a healthy and necessary part of growth.

Guilt is unhealthy. It wastes your energy with feelings of hurt that lie in the past, but that are experienced in the present. No amount of guilt can undo anything. As you learn from past mistakes, without feeling guilty, the tiger of the past will never raise its hungry head again.

2. Worry should be turned into work by planning for success.

How many minutes per day do you think you spend just worrying that you won't finish a project on time? Or that you won't have enough money to pay for the car insurance your teenage son needs?

Instead of worrying, take control! Chain yourself to your desk, go through your budget, brainstorm your project and write out a plan of action. Then start doing the tasks identified in your plan.

Peter Drucker, the management guru, stated: "The end result of planning should be tasks that can be implemented." When you plan your work and work your plan, the tiger of the future will never roar at you again.

As you quiet the tigers of guilt and worry, you'll become free to live in the moment by truly listening to conversations, thinking about what has been said, and responding in reflective, supportive ways. You'll be free to experience the moment by seeing the world around you: the colors, the sights, the sounds, and the beauty that exists. And you'll find yourself picking more strawberries.

Conditioning Exercises

1. Think of something in your past you worry about.

Does this event really matter now?
How can you let go of the guilt and/or worry this event is causing you?

2. Think of something in your future you're worrying about.

Take out a paper and pencil and make a plan for the successful completion of the project, or state what other direct action you will take to alleviate your worry.

Your mind should be quieted now that you have let go of the past and planned how to conquer your future. You can enjoy the quality living to be found in the present moment.

When The Winner Awakes

Do I use this in my own life? Yes, I do. When my kids were little, I worried constantly about their behavior. I wanted them to be perfect – always appropriate, straight-A students, great musicians and superstar sports figures. I wanted them to grow up to be the kind of superhuman hero that doesn't exist.

Every time they behaved like the little kids they were, it upset me and I worried that they wouldn't achieve perfection. I thought I could raise perfect children!

Then one day, I realized that they were perfect. I saw that they were perfectly human, perfectly wonderful individuals. What I needed to do was let go of the small daily conflicts that swirled around them when they were just kids being kids. I needed to provide direction, love them, and give them a positive, healthy framework within which they could grow.

After letting go of my worries, I watched with awe as my children began to turn into perfectly incredible people! At times, during their teen years, superhuman patience was required, but I gradually learned to replace worry with work, faith and tolerance.

Look at the four strategies listed on the following page and decide which strategy you would use to replace guilt and worry in each of the situations I describe.

1. LET GO

2. TAKE ACTION

3. HAVE FAITH

4. EXERCISE PATIENCE

THE PAST

Here are two situations about the past. Which strategy would you choose in order to replace guilt and worry?

1. You turned a report in two weeks ago with two errors that your spell check didn't catch.

2. You complained angrily to your team leader that your input was not requested about a decision one of your peers made on a project that affected you.

Now let's look at examples of choices you may have made. There are no "right" answers to these situations, but these examples will give you some general guidelines.

- ***Did you choose "let go"?***

With this strategy, you might say to yourself, "No, I won't beat myself up any more about this report. When the errors were pointed out to me, I immediately took the report back, revised the errors and submitted a correct version of the work. I'm not incompetent. I can let this go and concentrate on other work at hand."

- ***Did you choose "take action"?***

With the action strategy, you might apologize to your team leader for being angry about your peer. This alleviates the worry and anxiety of a past action into which you put too much venom.

Then you might open a calm and well-reasoned dialogue with your team leader, express your concerns and voice your opinions. Ask to be included the next time something comes up that affects your work projects. Taking this direct action will lessen the worry that the same thing will happen next week.

THE FUTURE

Here are three situations about the future:

1. You're worried about what will happen to you in your organization's merger.

2. You're afraid you won't make your quota.

3. You fear that you won't get the newly opened position, even though you're well qualified and perfectly capable of doing the job.

- ***Did you choose "take action"?***

Taking action would include analyzing the merger and deciding where your job position will fit. It may involve thinking about moves inside the company and positioning yourself in a different department.

You might also think about how your personal philosophies and skills fit with the new company. The next step would be either to have faith or look for a new job.

- ***Let's imagine you chose "take action" again.***

In this case, you might say to yourself: "I'm not leaving this desk until I've written plans that will help me achieve my goal." You would include in your written plan realistic figures and great detail about how you would make your quota.

You might ask yourself which clients are the best prospects and decide how much you can sell them. You might also devise a plan to get new prospects in the pipeline.

Once you produced a written plan, your mind would be calm and you wouldn't need so many Rolaids. You would simply go to work and put the plan into action.

- ***What if you chose a combination of these three strategies: take action, have faith, exercise patience.***

Great things happen to people who take action instead of sitting around waiting for good things to come to them. But there's another element to success that you need to accept: the prettiest girl does not always win the beauty contest. For instance, when it comes to gaining a promotion, you may not win the position for which you're qualified and that you feel you deserve.

You need to have faith that a better opportunity will come your way. You may also have to exercise patience. Sometimes great things take time to unfold. Life works to its own schedule, not necessarily to yours.

Take plenty of time for this aerobic. Allow the principles to sink deeply into your soul because it's important: If you're constantly trying to outrun the tigers of guilt and worry, you'll be unhappy, unproductive and tired.

You'll discover that every strategy you devise to rid yourself of guilt and worry involves *taking action* of some kind. You have to DO something to have mental and emotional health. So why not do it NOW?

"Life does not have to be perfect to be wonderful."

– Annette Funnicello

"Are you heading for the bridge with a parachute strapped to your back, or are you still standing by your car?"

THE SWINGING ROPE BRIDGE

DAILY MENTAL AEROBIC

Today I will live for what I truly value.

"The purpose of life is to live it, to taste each experience to the utmost, and to reach out, eagerly and without fear, for newer and richer experiences."

KARLA BRANDAU

I GREW UP IN IDAHO, RIGHT ACROSS THE SNAKE RIVER FROM Ontario, Oregon, where Ore-Ida, the famous potato company, was founded. Our home was near the spot where the Payette River tumbles into the Snake River.

My dad took frequent trips from our little town of New Plymouth to Cascade, where the Payette River has its origin at Cascade Lake. My sister and I loved to ride with Dad on these trips. It was fascinating to see the wild rapids and huge rocks of the powerful Payette River, then watch it diminish until it was a tame little stream.

At several points across the river, swinging rope bridges made it possible to cross from one side to the other. From the road, these bridges looked like so much fun that my sister and I begged Dad to stop and let us cross.

On one trip, our dream came true. Dad stopped the car and my sister and I jumped out. In great anticipation, we ran out onto the swinging rope bridge. Dad went ahead and waited for us on the other side.

We made it about a third of the way across when a strange thing happened. The water seemed to become angry as it swirled around below us. The little lilt of the bridge made us feel anything but secure. We became frozen with fright, our hands in a death grip on the rope rails.

From the far side, Dad encouraged us by telling us we could do it. We looked straight into his eyes and, steadily but surely, made our way across and into his arms.

If you saw a swinging rope bridge, would you jump out of your car to dance across it? Would you do it out of a sense of adventure? Would you do it as a dare? Would you do it for money? If I were on the opposite bank and offered you $50, would you cross? You may be enticed to cross a small river like the Payette for adventure, a dare, or money.

But let's change the scene. Upstream from where the Payette River merges with the Snake River is a canyon. It's not as massive as the Grand Canyon, but it's still pretty awesome. It was at the deepest point that Evil Knevil, the daredevil motorcyclist, made his famous attempt to jump the Snake River.

Out of a sense of adventure, would you bounce right out of your car and attempt to cross a flimsy little rope bridge across that canyon? Would you put your life in danger for a measly $50? For $500? Or $500,000? How about a big fat one million dollars, tax free? Are you heading for the bridge with a parachute strapped to your back, or are you still standing by your car?

Now, pretend with me. Pretend that I'm not a nice person. I'm a terrorist and I have a loved one of yours by the hair, promising to drop her or him into the deep canyon if you don't get across the bridge in three minutes flat. Now what's happening? Are you clamoring to get across?

Asking yourself what would motivate you to cross the swinging rope bridge is a process that helps you identify what you truly value.

Sure you value fun, adventure, and money. But you never know what your highest values are until you ask this question: "What would persuade me to cross the swinging rope bridge?"

Here is a fact that always sobers me: At the end of my life, the activities in which I invested my time and energy on a daily basis are the things for which I crossed the swinging rope bridge. This knowledge makes me choose more carefully.

Karla's Coaching Corner

The things you value most will probably fall into one or more of four categories:

1. ***Spiritual, Religious and Ethical Awareness***
2. ***Professional Performance***
3. ***Relationships***
4. ***Personal Development and Growth***

Here is a description of each category:

1. Spiritual, Religious and Ethical Awareness

All human beings possess a spiritual and ethical dimension. Some of us choose to express it in formal religion, while others manifest it in less formal ways.

Here are some examples of values that fall into this first category:

- Honesty
- Integrity
- Gratitude
- Honor
- Self-discipline
- Prayer
- Service to others
- Meditation

2. Professional Performance

To keep self-esteem at optimum functioning levels, the human psyche needs to be good at something. Exceptional professional performance gives humans a feeling of self-worth.

In addition, to have adequate food and shelter in today's world requires a certain level of professional competence. Examples of values in the professional performance category:

- Completing tasks on time
- Giving exceptional customer service
- Being a team player
- Being honest and candid

3. Relationships

Everybody has relationships – and they're usually in turmoil. Why? Because humans forget that the people they live with have innately different points of view, often strangely divergent values, and definitely dissimilar life experiences.

So values in this category are critical to the quality of life you lead. Value examples are:

- Improving communication with my spouse
- Making friendships at work to improve cooperation
- Spending time with my children
- Being neighborly
- Finding friends for stimulating conversations at professional association meetings

4. Personal Development and Growth

This is perhaps the most critical, and often the most neglected, of the value categories. It's not a selfish thing to take care of yourself, because personal development and growth make you a valued employee, a caring spouse and a connected parent. Examples of values in this category:

- Taking time for mental development
- Controlling emotions
- Exercising for increased stamina and energy
- Permitting time to rest and renew

Conditioning Exercises

From each of the four value categories listed above, think about what ***you*** value most.

What you value will probably be very different than what's written here and that's entirely appropriate. You must discover and articulate your own values.

Go through this evaluation process and identify those values for which you would cross the swinging rope bridge.

Begin to act on these values and, as you do, you'll find emotional calm and courage in the face of decisions.

I've watched little league baseball games when the tiny tykes got so confused that they just threw the ball around with no real purpose while the opposing team circled the bases and scored.

Sometimes you may feel as if you're doing the same thing with your life. You may be experiencing great confusion about where to invest your time and your energies, but don't worry. That will stop when the winner awakes.

When The Winner Awakes

You'll know this mental aerobic is working for you if you're able to make clear, focused choices in situations that present you with potential conflict, such as these:

- When an out-of-town business trip coincides with your child's first piano recital

- When you're asked to submit information on a report that you believe is inaccurate and should be more closely checked to avoid misleading figures

- When you're asked to take on an extra project at work that would provide high visibility, but that would necessitate postponing the vacation you promised to take with your spouse

- When your friend asks you to attend a social event you find boring

- When you're required to work on a Saturday to put out a proposal your team leader wants

There's no right or wrong answer to these situations. Only you can identify the right priorities and values in your life and only you can know what would persuade you to cross the swinging rope bridge.

A young man went to a fortune teller who looked into a crystal ball and said, "You'll be poor and unhappy until you're 45 years old."

The man was silently hoping that joy and riches would fill his life sooner rather than later. "Why 45? What will happen then?" he asked eagerly.

"Then you'll get used to it," came the reply.

The good things of life won't come to you automatically, but that doesn't mean you have to get used to poverty and unhappiness. If your crystal ball seems to be indicating unhappiness, change your future. Now!

And in your search for joy and happiness, remember that most of the best things in life don't cost a penny: a smile, the sunset, a hug, a cool breeze, a warm handshake and a compliment, to name just a few.

"Make the magic of joyful living part of your daily life by enjoying the things that are free."

– Karla Brandau

"Suddenly, the couch rose eerily into the air and floated out of the window, along with the TV, the remote control, and all of Henry's other possessions."

BREATHE IN, BREATHE OUT

DAILY MENTAL AEROBIC

I am an incredible human being!

"The trouble with most self-made men is that they stopped too soon."

ANONYMOUS

BREATHE IN SLOWLY TO THE COUNT OF THREE. BREATHE OUT slowly to the count of three. Now think about these three important questions:

1. ***Does your self-esteem equal your possessions?***
2. ***Does your self-esteem equal your performance on any given day?***
3. ***Does your self-esteem equal the praise you get?***

Breathe in slowly to the count of three. Breathe out slowly to the count of three. What answers did you give to the three questions above? Let's look at some of the issues they raise.

Does your self-esteem equal your possessions?

It's nice to have designer suits and multimillion-dollar homes, but how long did it take Hurricane Andrew to destroy 63,000 homes in Miami? Maybe five minutes at the most. If your entire self-esteem had been tied up in possessions that were destroyed by Hurricane Andrew, you would have been destroyed too.

Unless you're Henry, that is. After Henry's funeral, his wife and son were consoling each other in the living room when the window opened mysteriously.

Suddenly the couch rose eerily into the air and floated out of the window, along with the TV, the remote control and all of Henry's other possessions. "Oh, no!" cried Henry's wife. "He's taking them with him."

Does your self-esteem equal your performance on any given day?

It would be nice if we were a "high ten" every day, but we aren't. So don't let your self-esteem be tied to performance.

Here's an example: The son of a friend of mine wanted to remember his mom's birthday, so he came to her work place with a huge bouquet of flowers. As he wound his way through the building to her office, he gathered a following of curious people who wondered what kind of occasion warranted such a beautiful bouquet of flowers.

The son knocked on his mother's door. She looked up and stammered in utter disbelief, "Why John, what possessed you?"

John replied, "Well, Mom, I was going to bring you cigarettes for your birthday, but I remembered that you quit smoking. Then I was going to bring you wine, but I knew you were cutting back on drinking. Then I thought of candy, but realized you were trying to diet. So in the end I brought you flowers, because YOU STILL SMELL."

We aren't Bibles, encyclopedias, computers or robots. We are humans. We make mistakes and say things we later regret, much like John or the young lady I once interviewed for a job. Her resume was above average and her interview went well. As I looked at her application form, however, I noticed her answer to the last question on page four, "Who would you call in case of an emergency?" She had penciled in, "911?"

Does your self-esteem equal the praise you get?

Do you ever get enough praise or encouragement for the things you do? If you answered "yes," you're one in a million. The rest of us have to be very good at patting ourselves on the back mentally and emotionally.

So give this a try: Raise your right hand high above your head. Cross it over your shoulder. Now pat!

In case you're wondering what breathing has to do with self-esteem, the answer is that the very fact you breathe makes you an incredible human being.

When you wake up every morning, take a deep breath and reaffirm that you can handle all of the challenges the day offers. Reaffirm that you're a winner. Pat yourself on the back and make your self-esteem irrepressible.

Karla's Coaching Corner

Self-esteem is just what it says: SELF-esteem. If self-esteem isn't generated from within but by what other people tell you, it becomes OTHER-esteem; it's not SELF-worth, but OTHER-worth. Build your self-esteem by doing the things listed on the next page.

1. Verbalize your talents and strengths.

Your self-esteem will improve if you say good things about yourself out loud, such as:

- I have a great smile.
- I'm caring and friendly.
- I'm good with computers.
- I can analyze well.

If you feel slightly embarrassed when you first try this, don't worry – it's understandable. Some people have an innate dislike of drawing attention to themselves, while others were told as a child, "Don't be a braggart." Be persistent and you'll find this technique working for you.

2. Take direct action when you have a problem.

When you have a difficult problem staring you in the face, don't sit around immobilized by worry, or start pouting and whining, "Why me?" Use constructive coping instead. Constructive coping involves confronting the problem directly. It's task-relevant and action-oriented. It entails a conscious effort to evaluate your options rationally so you can solve your problems.

Whether the problem you face is a misunderstanding with someone or a distasteful project your team leader gave you, take direct action. Do something. Talk out your differences of opinion.

Brainstorm with a friend on any project that's overwhelming you. Whatever you do, don't procrastinate. Putting off a hard task only makes it harder to take action.

3. Give up perfectionism.

The next time you watch TV, pay attention to the perfection projected in commercials. You'll see ads for perfect cars, ice cream, soap, vacations, jeans, waxed floors and toilet bowls. TV commercials would have you think it's possible to reach perfection.

In reality, we live in an imperfect world where cars break down, some soaps make your skin itch, vacations are plagued by sunburn and mosquitoes, jeans don't fit properly, and people slip on waxed floors.

So, regardless of what copywriters claim or TV commercials depict, nothing is perfect. There are no perfect kids, spouses, peers or dogs. You'll be happier if you don't expect perfection from everyone you meet.

4. Make yourself happy.

You can only make yourself happy. You can't make other people happy.

Before you learn this principle, you'll probably spend many quality hours trying to make someone happy, especially if it's someone dear to you, such as spouse, kids or friends. But it's impossible.

The only thing you can do to affect the optimism of others is to master your own optimism.

Learn how to be happy on a daily basis and you'll free yourself to create an environment of support for other people. As you encourage them, they will find their own happiness. When two or more happy people share life, true magic happens.

5. Make a "victory film."

Think back to the times when you received praise for your work and the times you were performing "in the zone." You can improve your self-esteem by remembering those times of excellence and building them into your own mental movie.

When you feel down, stressed, or pressured by inadequacies, run the film in your mind. It will give you new determination to keep climbing.

6. Let each new day have a life of its own.

You aren't your behaviors. Every morning is a fresh start. You can be anything you want to be today. You don't have to be what you were yesterday. Just breathe in slowly and breathe out slowly. Affirm your abilities, follow these six tips, and make it a great day.

Conditioning Exercises

1. ***What are your best qualities?***
2. ***Why do people like you?***
3. ***What events would be in your victory film?***

If you have trouble with these questions, call a friend and ask them to imagine they're filling out an award form for you. Ask them for their feedback on your strengths.

After you have made mental notes of your best qualities, start recording the events that made you feel proud, the ones that belong in your victory film. Include more than accolades and awards, though. Also include the moments you smiled in the face of trouble or cheerfully greeted someone who knowingly said unkind things about you.

Now breathe in and breathe out freely. Undoubtedly, you have discovered once again what a truly incredible human being you are.

When The Winner Awakes

You'll have absorbed the essence of this aerobic when you can cope with a day when the following kinds of things happen:

- Before giving a presentation, you're so nervous that your thought processes are being disrupted
- Milk gets spilled on your architectural drawings that you must present to the client tomorrow
- The dog eats your best shoe
- Your child's teacher calls for the second time this week
- Your administrative assistant is ill
- You have a knock-down, drag-out verbal battle with the team member who is heading up the project to which you're assigned

After this kind of a day, you may think you'll need Excedrin PM to get to sleep. Not so. Find a quiet place, breathe deeply and play your victory film in your mind. Say to yourself, "These things are temporary. Tomorrow is a new day. I'll just go to sleep. I'm an incredible person."

You'll wake up in the morning ready to face and conquer your problems.

"Winners bring reality up to their vision. Losers bring their vision down to reality."

– Chuck Knox

"They went around the neighborhood collecting broken bicycles and pulling them out of the trash. Soon I had spokes, handlebars, seats and greasy chains all over my carport."

AEROBIC FOUR **4**

THE BEAUTY MAKE-OVER

DAILY
MENTAL AEROBIC

Today I will maintain internal beauty.

"When you find the way, others will find you. Passing by on the road, they will be drawn to your door. The way that cannot be heard will be echoed in your voice. The way that cannot be seen will be reflected in your eyes."

ROBIN LAO-TZU, IN THE TAO-TE CHING

ONE DAY, I RECEIVED A LETTER INVITING ME TO MY 20-YEAR high school reunion. I won't tell you when I received the invitation, only that I did! I was very excited at the prospect of seeing old friends and my mind flooded with memories.

Then I looked in the mirror and stopped short. "Oh my word," I said to myself. "Look at the wrinkles. Look at the bags under my eyes. Everyone will be able to tell that I've aged." I began to feel depressed.

So I went to the mall and ended up at a beauty counter with a Mrs. Fields white chocolate, macadamia nut cookie in my hand. The young woman at the counter said, "Hey lady, would you like a beauty make-over?" Would I ever! I knew instinctively that a beauty make-over was exactly what I needed.

Two hours later, I walked away from that beauty counter swinging two large bags – you know what it takes to be beautiful. I walked out into the mall, looking and feeling gorgeous. I wanted to shout: "Move over, Julia Roberts. Watch out, Cindy Crawford. Here comes Karla!"

I marched confidently down the mall to look for a dress befitting my new face. I walked into Macy's and began to make my way past the beauty counters toward the dress department. The first sales assistant who saw me cried out, "Hey lady, would you like a beauty make-over?"

Ouch! That hurt, but I steeled myself, looked her in the eye and said, "Honey, when I was your age I was a diamond in the rough. Now I'm cut, polished and beautiful. If you have two hours, I'll tell you just how I've been polished all these years."

Karla's Coaching Corner

When you came into the world, you were beautiful, both inside and out. But, if you're anything like me, you spend more time thinking about how to maintain your physical beauty than you do thinking about how to maintain your inner beauty. That goes for men as well as women.

How do you maintain inner beauty? By cultivating

positive character traits, loving other people and being optimistic. In the book *The Prophet,* Kahlil Gibran writes:

"The appearance of things changes according to the emotions, and thus we see magic and beauty in them, while the magic and beauty are really in ourselves."

Did you catch what Kahlil Gibran is saying? I had to read it two or three times and let the words sink in deep. What finally dawned on me was the truth that other people remain constant. Whether I like them or dislike them is up to me. It's my viewpoint of other people that determines whether or not they're beautiful. It's my mood on a particular day that creates a synergistic relationship.

If this is true, it's up to you to create happiness in your own mind. It's up to you to put magic in the world and to see beauty in the people around you. You can gain inner strength to do this and learn to refresh your inner beauty on a daily basis by doing these things:

1. Cultivate positive character traits, such as honesty and integrity.

You'll be popular when you prove that you can keep your word and deliver on your promises. Every time you're true to your deeply held values, your self-esteem increases.

When I started playing tennis, it was impressed on me that if the ball hits even a portion of the line on its way out, it's deemed to be "in bounds." A few years later, this rule became the focus of a remarkable display of integrity.

At the French Open in 1982, Matts Wilander had reached match point in the championship game. If he won the next point, he would win the title. When the ball came across the net, the umpire called it out, which meant Wilander had won the championship. But Wilander knew the ball had touched the line, so he marched over to the chair umpire and said, "I will not win this way. That ball was good."

On his insistence, the point was played over. Wilander won it, thus taking the French Open title with his integrity intact.

2. Demonstrate your love for others by reserving judgment and by showing them respect.

My son Mark taught me a valuable lesson about judging others. When he was about 10 years old, he and his friends decided to go into the business of fixing bicycles. They went around the neighborhood collecting broken bicycles and pulling them out of the trash. Soon I had spokes, handlebars, seats and greasy chains all over my carport. It resembled a bicycle graveyard.

I looked at the mess and said, "Mark, you have to clean this up. We'll be thought of as junky people." Without any hesitation, he looked at me and said, "I don't think people should be judged by what they look like." Even at his young age, he knew that judging people would be wrong. I was awed by his insight.

Withholding judgment and extending respect are important skills taught by Mary Kay Ash, President of Mary Kay Cosmetics. She tells her sales consultants to visualize a sign around every person's neck that says, "Make Me Feel Important," and exhorts those consultants to do something to make people feel that way.

Taking respect to an even higher level, Mother Theresa said that we should love each other with a tender and most personal love, just like God loves each of us. To love others in a nonjudgmental, respectful way makes you beautiful inside.

3. Be optimistic.

Nobody, I repeat nobody, likes to be around a negative person. My good friend Jane Riley says, "Don't walk away from negative people. RUN!"

The negative and the positive are parallel forces. They flow around you every minute of the day and you decide which you will be – negative or positive. It takes practice, but you can become a person who looks out the window and sees birds, butterflies and blue sky, not specks and smudges on the window pane.

In some circumstances, being positive takes a major effort, like the time we went camping with some friends when our kids were little. Much to our chagrin, it started raining on the first day.

By the third day, I'd had enough. Clothes were muddy, bedding was soggy and I had run out of games to entertain a four-year-old and a toddler in a two-person tent. I was hoarse from repeated renditions of *Itsy Bitsy Spider.* I was packing to leave!

Then I heard my friend singing while she started a fire to cook breakfast. Even though the rain was still falling, she sang *Oh What a Beautiful Morning* as she worked. "Yeah, right," I thought. "Give me a break."

And a break was exactly what I got. Soon the rain turned to a gentle mist and the sun started to peek through a cloud. I stopped packing and decided to give it another try. It turned out to be a beautiful day and I enjoyed the rest of the vacation, thanks to my friend's optimism.

Conditioning Exercises

Contemplate your inner beauty.
If you were alone with yourself,
would it be pleasant?

Think of a character trait you would like
to improve, such as being more tactful.
Where can you go to learn about tact?
How can you practice it?

Think of someone you don't like.
What "smudges" have you seen on this person?
Can you look through the window of their soul?
Do you see a different person?

Think of something you have a negative
opinion about. If you look at it in
another way, can you find
a positive side?

If you can maintain integrity, respect others and choose the positive, your internal beauty will shine brightly. When it does, you'll never need a beauty make-over again.

When The Winner Awakes

Here's how you'll know when this aerobic has become second nature:

An angry friend comes to you, having just been told she is rude. She asks you, "Is it so?" This is the moment of truth. You think she is too brash sometimes. You could say, "Yup. You're one of the rudest people I've ever met."

Instead you say, "In certain situations, you have the potential to come on pretty strong. Some people may see that as rudeness." Then if you add a friendly smile and a gentle nod of the head, you may open a discussion of her situation. Since you have shown that you can handle the problem in an honest but kind way, you'll be making progress in developing a new character trait: Tact.

Next take a situation where you feel negatively toward a person. Stephen Covey tells the story of a man and his six children on the subway in New York City. The children were going crazy, running up and down the aisles and creating havoc. The other passengers on the train were annoyed and wondered why the man was just sitting there as if in a stupor, ignoring his rampaging children.

One especially impatient passenger could contain himself no longer. In a brusque tone of voice, he asked the father to calm down his children. The father looked at the man and said, "Oh, I'm terribly sorry. I just lost my wife to cancer. I guess I'm not really thinking straight."

If this story has the same effect on you that it had on me, you won't judge people so quickly in the future. Instead, you'll make an effort to see their situations and understand their perspectives. And then there's the value of optimism. Nothing makes you glow more than an optimistic and hopeful spirit. Nothing makes you more undesirable than a negative attitude.

Let's take the business world as an example. Some real-life applications of this aerobic might be PM and AM which, in this case, stand for Pre-Merger and After-Merger.

Mergers aren't going away, they're increasing. When you're involved in a merger, you need a defense mechanism. You need to look for the positive in the new organization, the new manager, or the new benefits package. To increase your job security, you need to be the one offering new ideas and presenting solutions to conflicts.

The same can apply to your personal life. Let's say your office is relocating, which requires you to move to a new neighborhood. Yes, you have to find new doctors, new dentists, and memorize the aisles in a new grocery store. You have to find new shortcuts to your favorite places.

This makes extra work for you and your family, but you don't let it get you down. You maintain an optimistic attitude by thinking about the new friends you'll meet and the new experiences that will come your way. You increase your positive attitude by enjoying the act of selecting a new house plan and choosing new carpets, wallpaper and paint.

Seeing new adventures in situations that circumstances forced upon you will save you untold negative emotions and preserve your internal beauty.

"I have an everyday religion that works for me: Love yourself first and everything else falls into line. You really have to love yourself to get anything done in this world."

–Lucille Ball

"Obsolescence infiltrates every business and every life like a stealth bomber."

AEROBIC FIVE **5**

THE LIGHT BULB

DAILY
MENTAL AEROBIC
Today I will learn something new.

"You think you understand the situation,
but what you don't understand is
that the situation just changed."

PUTNAM INVESTMENTS ADVERTISEMENT

A COUPLE OF YEARS AGO, I ATTENDED A MEETING IN Tennessee where a speaker told the audience that he once had a job he enjoyed very much. He had been a night watchman for ten years and was confident that he would be in that job for another ten years.

Then one afternoon he went to work and found that he had been replaced by a light bulb. His company installed new electricals at the facility, put up a lamp post, screwed in a light bulb, and suddenly there was no more need for a night watchman. The audience began to chuckle at this and so did I, until I realized it was not funny.

This man had been caught in the trap of obsolescence. In reality, you never know what kind of technology might replace your physical actions, be it robot, computer, or procedure. Obsolescence infiltrates every business and every life like a stealth bomber.

Bill Gates, cofounder and president of Microsoft, writes in *The Road Ahead,* "What seems the perfect business plan or latest technology today may soon be as out-of-date as records, the eight-track tape player, the vacuum-tube television, or the mainframe computer." The only insurance against obsolescence is using your mind, developing creative talent, having original ideas to solve problems and making a daily commitment to invest in self-development.

Karla's Coaching Corner

When I went back to my 20-year high school reunion, I noticed that one of my classmates had not changed one iota from the day we graduated. This said a lot about her weight, but not much about her hairstyle! Can you visualize a 20-year-old hairdo? She needed to use a process I call "Creative Abandonment."

Creative Abandonment reminds you to examine your life, habits and attitudes to see what things need to be creatively abandoned before they become obsolete.

To stay current in today's world, you must be in perpetual motion – constantly reshaping, shifting and flexing to new conditions. A necessary tool to help you stay current is to develop what I call "Triple Vision."

I learned about this phenomenon while watching a football game. The receiver dodged his opponents, kept his eye on the ball, and made a spectacular catch. But he came down one yard out of bounds. He had failed to keep his eye on the playing field. He lacked Triple Vision.

When I started playing tennis, I had to use the same skill. I found I won more points if I directed the ball away from my opponent. To do this, I had to be able to see the court, the ball and my opponent. I had to have Triple Vision.

You can increase your job security and give extra value to your employer if you use Triple Vision at work. Determine to see what the marketplace is (the court), how your organization's products fit (the ball), and what your competitors are doing (the opponent).

To develop Triple Vision, make a commitment to read industry-specific magazines and newsletters. Peruse the newspaper. Join professional associations and talk to experts in your field. As you do these things, you'll know instinctively what's becoming obsolete.

To develop Triple Vision and creatively abandon what's becoming outdated takes concerted effort when you're preoccupied with the narrow focus of today's tasks. If you do develop Triple Vision, however, you'll experience an amazing return on investment for the time expended.

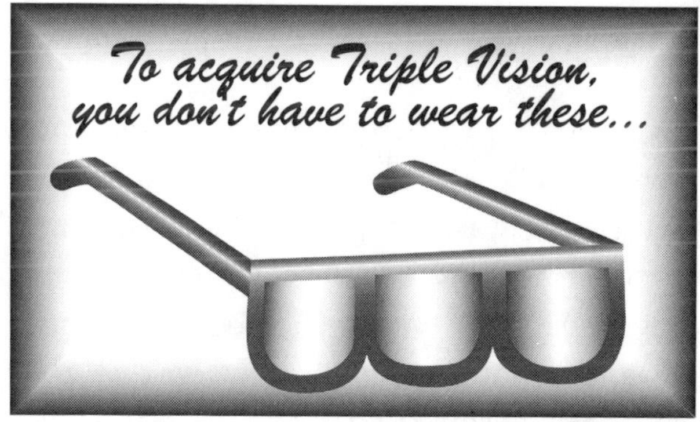

Conditioning Exercises

Tomorrow, when you're closing out the day and getting ready to go home from work, take about five minutes to think about something you did during the day that's becoming obsolete.

After dinner, contemplate anything that's happening in your personal life to make you obsolete and out of date.

Act! Creatively abandon it all!

Once you have creatively abandoned the identified items, you'll have room in your brain for the new. Learn it now!

When The Winner Awakes

I knew that I had to creatively abandon some of my learning when I discovered that high school students don't take "typing" any more. They take "keyboarding." It takes a lot of concentration to use the new term "keyboarding" and not revert back to "typing," expecting younger people to understand what I mean. Similarly, I've also had to replace the word "record" with "CD."

Learning how to use the remote control, understanding all the bells and whistles on your new cell phone, or using debit cards instead of a checkbook, are all signs of your determination to learn new things. Facing these learning challenges will keep your life from becoming stagnant.

In your work life, you may be using 3 x 5 cards and an accordion file to keep up with contacts and tickler items. How about switching to an up-to-date contact software package? Yes, there's a learning curve with new software, and you have to pay for all the upgrades, but the time and money will be well spent. Your investment increases your chances of not being replaced by a light bulb.

Do you still resist selling yourself and your products through a Web site? Internet e-commerce is the future.

I challenge you to embrace new technology and let go of habitual out-of-date ways of doing things. Learn something new every day and your mental toughness will command respect from all those with whom you associate.

"Where there is an open mind, there will always be a frontier."

– Charles F. Kettering

"Now you're ready to work behind the counter."

AEROBIC SIX **6**

WORKING IN THE ZONE

DAILY MENTAL AEROBIC

Today I will live in the emotion of love.

"The things which hurt, instruct."

Benjamin Franklin

Tennis Great Arthur Ashe Said That On The Day He Won Wimbledon, he could have beaten anyone. He was playing in "The Zone."

Athletes understand what The Zone is, but they don't talk about it much. When they're in The Zone, they know how each play will unfold, where the ball will bounce, and where to move to make the next play.

One of the ways you can live in The Zone is to raise the emotional level at which you function when you experience three key emotions – hate, duty and love.

Ken Norton, a friend of mine, tells a story about moving from hate, through duty, to love. When working his way through college, he applied for a job at a sandwich shop. The owner, Mr. Whitehead, told Ken that his first job would be making sandwiches.

On his first day in his new job, Ken came in to work through the back door of the sandwich shop. As Ken crossed the sticky floor, Mr. Whitehead stopped him next to a sink filled with dirty, greasy dishes. "This is where you'll start," he said.

Ken was mad. He pointed out to Mr. Whitehead that he had been hired to make sandwiches. Mr. Whitehead responded by saying, "Well, this is the work that needs to be done today. Take it or leave it."

Although he was filled with hate, Ken started to wash the dishes, because he desperately needed the money. He worked slowly, but methodically.

The next morning, he sighed and once again plunged his hands dutifully into the wash water. Around noon, he began to whistle and quickened the pace of his work. A few minutes later, Mr. Whitehead poked his head around the door and asked, "Norton, are you all right?"

"Yes, sir," Ken replied amiably. "I just decided that if I had to do this, I might as well learn to love it."

A few minutes later, Mr. Whitehead stepped through the door with a clean white apron in his hands and said, "Now you're ready to work behind the counter."

KARLA'S COACHING CORNER

In only 24 hours, Ken Norton went through the three emotions I mentioned earlier – hate, duty and love. As a normal human being living a perfectly normal day, you'll also experience these three emotions.

There are tasks you hate to do, but you do them because of the fear of negative consequences. There are tasks you do out of duty, maybe because they're part of the job description, or maybe because you have been raised with the work ethic that employees should give an honest day's work for an honest day's pay.

However, the ultimate experience in productivity is to work in the emotion of love. Here, work is effortless and feels like play. You're working in The Zone. You have tapped into your greatest potential. Michael Jordan calls The Zone his "fourth gear."

The Zone phenomenon has been described by Professor Mihaly Csikszentmihalyi, former chairman of the Department of Psychology at the University of Chicago, as the "Flow State." This term may more nearly describe the business experience as opposed to the sports experience.

When you're in The Zone, or the Flow State, you're totally absorbed in a particular activity, and this state of total absorption precludes doubt, anxiety and fear. You're oblivious to all distractions. Your state of mind is characterized by self-trust, enjoyment and focused relaxation. Your mind is creative and innovative. You have increased problem-solving abilities and decision-making skills. On this level, energy and enthusiasm replenish themselves daily.

Golf legend Jack Nicklaus once observed, "Golf is 90 percent mental." Winning in the business field may be 95% mental. To win the mental game in business and perform in The Zone, you need to raise the emotion of hate to duty and raise the emotion of duty to love, just like Ken Norton did.

Why is this so important? Once again, I quote Jack Nicklaus: "I'm a firm believer in the theory that people only do their best at things they truly enjoy. It's difficult to excel at something you don't like."

How can you transform your energy from hate to love? Take a task that you hate to do but do out of fear and try to dump, discard, dissolve, or disintegrate it. If none of those strategies work, elevate hate to duty by changing your attitude and your internal self-talk.

Say to yourself, "Yes, this is inconvenient. Yes, this is crummy. But I *can* do it and I *will* do it."

When you do what you love, even if you arrived there by changing your inner dialogue, you'll find self-replenishing motivation. You'll find the enthusiasm to break the pull of gravity under your bed in the morning.

Who knows? You might get promoted to work behind whatever represents the counter for you.

CONDITIONING EXERCISES

Think of a task you hate to do.

How can you reduce, eliminate, or minimize the effects on your productivity? By changing your attitude and your internal self-talk, can you move from hate to duty?

Think of a task you do out of duty.

By changing your attitude and your internal self-talk, can you raise the emotion to love? Or is it a task that's routine and so the emotion of duty is sufficient?

Think of a task you love to do.

Do it. Make time for it. Clear your schedule for it. Find a way to make money by doing what you love.

Make a commitment to spend a portion of every day working in the emotion of love. If you do, you'll be working at the highest level of productivity and enthusiasm.

When The Winner Awakes

It's a given that there's something to hate about every job. For some people, the things to hate about a job could be as high as 20%. If it goes over 20%, you'll be in trouble mentally and emotionally. Eventually you'll be in physical trouble as well, because the mental and emotional parts of your psyche affect you physically.

To preserve your health, take the thing you hate to do and change the emotion. For instance, do you hate to:

- Attend your spouse's office party?
- Fill out your expense report?
- Complete quarterly reports?
- Wait for answers so you can complete a project?
- Learn a new computer program?
- Switch vendors?
- Find consultants?
- Hire new employees?
- Clean your bathroom?
- Wash your clothes?
- Take clothes to the dry cleaners?
- Wait in line at the grocery store?

For the things you truly hate to do, find ways around them. For example, if you hate shopping, you may decide to shop at 7:00 AM or 11:00 PM when there are far fewer people in line. Or you may decide to hire someone to take your clothes to the dry cleaners and clean your bathroom.

When it comes to hiring new people, finding consultants and switching vendors, a playful attitude can work. Make it a game. For example, you can play "hide and seek." Imagine that the new people you need are in hiding and you're seeking them.

Look for the benefits of finishing a particular task. For instance, visualize the efficiency found in learning a new computer program. Another strategy is to give yourself a reward after you do your quarterly reports or fill out your expense report. The reward can be as simple as going to Ben and Jerry's for your favorite ice cream or scheduling a game with your favorite golf buddy.

How about your spouse's office party? It takes true mental toughness to paste on that support-your-spouse smile and tell yourself, "I'm gonna love this!" Believe it and you'll feel the winner awakening!

"Love those who deserve it as if there is no tomorrow. Because when you get right down to it, there isn't."

– Anonymous

*"Rosie changed.
He started giving 110% on every play."*

AEROBIC SEVEN **7**

MERLIN AND ROSIE

DAILY MENTAL AEROBIC

Today I will give life 110%.

"The future is bought with the present."

SAMUEL JOHNSON

SEVERAL YEARS AGO, MY NEPHEW GRADUATED FROM WEISER High School. Merlin Olsen was the commencement speaker. Merlin spoke about his time as a player with the Los Angeles Rams. He told us about the time when his teammate, Rosie Greer, wasn't giving 100% effort.

Merlin and two other teammates saw how Rosie's lack of effort was hurting the team, so they decided to act. The three of them talked to Rosie, but he denied any lack of effort. He said, "Naw, you guys are wrong. I give 100% all the time."

Merlin and his teammates didn't let the matter drop. They arranged for the next practice to be videotaped. Then they set up the VCR in Rosie's room so that he had to watch the tape before he went to sleep.

At around 2 AM in the morning, Merlin was awakened by someone shaking him. It was Rosie. He said, "You were right. I wasn't giving 100%."

Rosie changed. He started giving *110%* on every play, not only in actual games, but in practice too. His performance was phenomenal. Two weeks later, Rosie was lying in a hospital bed with a torn Achilles tendon. The doctors told him he would never play football again. When Merlin went to visit Rosie, his injured teammate looked up sadly and said, "Why didn't I learn to give 110% nine years ago?"

Karla's Coaching Corner

When I studied history in high school, I was always impressed by the contributions certain brilliant people had made to the world: Ben Franklin, Mahatma Gandhi, Winston Churchill, Albert Einstein, and Albert Schweitzer to name just a few.

Knowing the value of their contributions should have inspired me to work harder, but I allowed myself to become discouraged by the feeling that the achievements of past giants were unattainable to me.

It's true that intellect is a factor, but in the process of contemplating success, I learned that extraordinary achievement takes an ordinary commitment to give 110% every day. Successful people often say, "Yes, I'm an overnight success, but it took me 20 years to become one."

Their break came through giving 110% effort, persevering, focusing on the project at hand and sticking with it until the job was done.

Beverly Sills, the metropolitan opera star, said, "Some singers make it with ten roles. I learned a hundred! If mine was an overnight success, it was the longest day's journey you ever saw!"

George Bernard Shaw said, "People are always blaming their circumstances for what they are. I don't believe in circumstances. The people who get on in this world are the people who get up and look for the circumstances they want and if they can't find them, make them."

I love the book *As A Man Thinketh* by the British author James Allen. My favorite part is where the author shows that you can break free of seemingly difficult circumstances:

"Your circumstances may be uncongenial, but they shall not long remain so if you but perceive an ideal and strive to reach it. Here is a youth hard pressed by poverty and labor, confined long hours in an unhealthy workshop; unschooled and lacking all the arts of refinement.

"But he dreams of better things; he thinks of intelligence, of refinement, of grace and beauty. He conceives of, mentally builds up, an ideal condition of life; the vision of which takes possession of him; unrest urges him to action and he utilizes all his spare time and means, small though they are, to the development of his latent powers and resources. Very soon so altered has his mind become that the workshop can no longer hold him. It has become so out of harmony with his mentality that it falls out of his life as a garment is cast aside and, with the growth of opportunities which fit the scope of his expanding power, he passes out of it forever."

Making your own circumstances is like putting on a full-court press in basketball. It's having self-discipline. It's getting up early in the morning and giving up an hour of TV every day for self-development. It's being fully present and concentrating on the task at hand.

Through this process, you create your own destiny, become your own overnight success and pass out of the "unhealthy workshop" forever.

If you choose to create your own luck, keep these two points in mind:

1. Never give minimal effort while waiting for your "break" to arrive.

Giving minimal effort is like punching in on the time clock every day, doing just enough work so they don't fire you, and enduring a boring day. Typically, people who do this get angry when they don't get promoted. Then they complain that they're being discriminated against. But, in reality, they have just been marking time.

I challenge you not to mark time, but to mark the world in a positive way. Move forward in any way you can. When obstacles present themselves, go under, through, around, or over. Whatever it takes, just go.

Several years ago, I met a young lady who had majored in broadcast journalism. When she graduated, no one would hire her in her hometown of Los Angeles. Even though she didn't want to leave LA, she took a job with a small cable station in Atlanta. She interviewed, hosted and produced – whatever the job required.

Recently, she received a lucrative offer from a station in Los Angeles and returned home in triumph. This young lady had the positive character trait of ambition – the desire to succeed. Ambition permitted her to learn faster, work smarter, do better, go farther and achieve more in a shorter amount of time than other less goal-directed peers.

Along with ambition, she had enthusiasm and a passion for her work. She was willing to take on the risk of a challenging assignment and willingly went that extra mile.

If you can implement these qualities, you'll never have to worry about getting a break. You'll get all the breaks you want.

2. Work more, procrastinate less.

When I was a young girl, I was taught to work. We had beautiful wood floors in our family home. At least they were beautiful after my sister Marianne and I had waxed them *by hand,* using what my mother called "elbow grease." We also weeded the garden, mowed the lawn, milked cows and baled hay. Gradually, we acquired the habit of working hard.

Academy Award winner Tommy Lee Jones was also taught to work hard as a youth. He told reporter Gail Buchalter, "My family were all hard-working people. I take pride in it. It wasn't particularly talked about – it's just something I watched my father do. Now, I never sit still and do nothing. I always have a lot of things that need to be done."

Golden Globe award winner Lauren Bacall had a similar experience. In an interview with Dotson Rader, Lauren said, "My mother was the greatest example to me of anyone I've ever known. She worked hard all her life and she was the one who set my values. I wasn't brought up as a society girl to go to balls, be a debutante, marry into money and the social set, and go to parties. No one in my family lived like that. And I never wanted to live like that. I was brought up to believe in work."

If we know that work is such an important principle, and that without it you can't achieve anything, why do we procrastinate? Procrastination can be a problem in any area of life, from balancing your budget or finishing a work project, to making out a will or getting a passport.

Procrastination is related to indecisiveness. It creates anxiety and guilt. Behavior patterns can become so ingrained and familiar that you don't recognize you have a problem. But, like a band of termites in a wooden house, procrastination chomps away at your time and your achievements.

Procrastination may have started the first time your mother told you to clean your room *"TODAY, OR ELSE."* In an effort to be your own person and start making your own decisions, maybe you rebelled and thought, "I'll clean it when I'm ready... maybe about midnight."

Be aware of the first signs of procrastination: feeling overwhelmed, feeling extreme pressure, or feeling like you'll fail on a high-priority project. Procrastination becomes your way to escape the stressful thoughts and emotions that accompany such situations. It helps you to ignore painful things. You delay tasks and goals in favor of less-pressing, lower-priority items, or highly pleasurable pursuits such as a trip to the break room, ordering pizza, or having a donut with your coffee.

You don't procrastinate to be ornery or because you're lazy or irrational. You procrastinate because it makes sense to you at that moment. If you procrastinate, it insulates you from criticism, failure and the need to do things perfectly.

Remember that talent is 99% perspiration, not procrastination. If you can overcome the human tendency to procrastinate, you'll prosper, because success is determined by action, not birthright.

The first three letters of triumph are t-r-i, which sounds like "try." Persistent trying, combined with 110% effort, will give you 110% rewards. Work more and procrastinate less and you'll never have to say, "Why didn't I learn to give 110% nine years ago?"

Conditioning Exercises

Think of a part of your life, either personal or professional, where you're not achieving the results you want. Are you giving only minimal effort and/or procrastinating?

Why is it important for you to improve this area of your life?

Now think of three ways in which you could give 110% effort that would make a significant improvement.

The real magic will begin in your life and your future will be bright, if you take the present moment and give 110% effort to just one of your ideas.

When The Winner Awakes

You'll know you have caught the vision and spirit of giving 110% if you:

- Persevere on a project even if you have to chain yourself to the desk
- Break a 40-hour job down into 30-minute increments
- Make the toughest job #1 on your "To-Do" list instead of #10
- Set mini-goals and deadlines to finish a project
- Give yourself rewards when you meet your mini-deadlines
- Tackle jobs you fear with determination to complete them in a timely way

Another sign you understand the 110% principle is that you're willing to work hard. I have a friend who has interviewed hundreds of people for jobs in the international company for which he works. He has a unique question that he uses in interviews.

At the end of the interview, he leans back casually in his big blue leather chair, gives an encouraging smile and asks, "What was your favorite part-time job as a teenager?" My friend maintains that, if they worked hard in part-time jobs as a teenager, candidates will have developed the kind of work ethic he wants in his corporation. If they reply, "Oh, I didn't work in high school" or say, "I hated them all," their resumes go to the bottom of the pile.

Keep yourself at the top of the stack. Be willing to work hard and carry yourself with businesslike resolve. You'll find life gives you back 110%.

Graduate from procrastination and minimal effort to giving 110%.

"While these raw recruits suffer from the fear of failure, they also suffer from the fear of success."

AEROBIC EIGHT **8**

HANDS ON THE OUTSIDE

DAILY MENTAL AEROBIC

Today I will put my hands on the outside.

"There is always room at the top, but the elevator is not running. You must walk up the stairs on your own feet."

DAVID STARR JORDAN

A FEW YEARS AGO, I WAS ASKED TO RUN A SERIES OF productivity programs for the Army at Fort Benning, home of the 101st Airborne Division. As I taught them about time management, I learned a lot about paratroopers and how new recruits approach the open door of opportunity to make their first jump.

Understand that, for these new recruits, the door of opportunity opens at an elevation of about 2,000 feet, and the plane is flying at about 150 miles per hour. Why someone would want to leave a perfectly safe airplane under these conditions puzzles anyone except a psychologist and the jumpmaster.

Here's something else to think about: While these raw recruits suffer from the fear of failure, they also suffer from the fear of success. If they can make a successful jump in sunny Columbus, Georgia, where do they get to do it next? Behind enemy lines in the dead of winter, perhaps?

During this project, I came to understand that there are two types of raw recruits. The first type approaches the door in hesitation mode. When they get to the door, they put their hands on the INSIDE of the plane, right where they have been told *not* to put them. If they look anywhere, they look down.

Picture these recruits standing at the door, shaking. Want to know how they leave the plane? They're pushed out by the jumpmaster! As a result of this halfhearted exit, recruits increase the chances of their parachute malfunctioning and failing to open properly. After watching their buddies get pushed out, the recruits still waiting to jump are transformed into a second type of raw recruit.

These new types of recruits approach the open door of opportunity determined to leave the plane under their own power. They choose to do the things that will ensure a successful jump and a safe landing. They place their hands on the OUTSIDE of the plane and they do it for two reasons.

First, they have been told to do so in order to maximize their safety when leaving the plane. Second, they place their hands on the outside for mental and emotional reasons. They are erasing, eradicating, obliterating and removing any notion that they will change their minds and stay inside the plane.

Instead of looking down in anticipation of failure, these types of recruits look up and find themselves a friendly cloud as a goal. At the signal, they take a deep breath, bend their knees, focus their energies and make a giant leap. They execute the proper count, pull the ripcord and have the exhilarating experience of floating down to the ground.

Karla's Coaching Corner

In a similar way to those paratroopers, you stand at the open door of opportunity every morning. Are your hands on the inside or the outside? Do you embrace the new day and the changes and challenges it might bring? Or do you resist? Are you afraid of what you will face?

Many people place their hands on the inside and let problems, criticism and fear of failure dominate their thoughts. To change this, you have to come to grips with failure and realize that it doesn't exist. Can you think of a time in your life that you *totally* failed at something? You may not have performed to the level you wanted, or that others expected, but total failure in anything is rare. The fear of failure, however, is real and is a crippling emotion.

Nathaniel Hawthorne lost his position in the Custom House at Salem, Massachusetts. He went home utterly defeated and told his wife that he was a total failure. To his amazement, she greeted his dismal news with delight and said, "Now you can write your book." Hawthorne sat down and wrote *The Scarlet Letter*, still considered by many critics as the greatest novel ever written in our country.

Dr. Wayne Dyer says this about fear of failure: "You may be surprised to hear this, but failure does not exist. Failure is simply someone else's opinion of how a certain act should have been completed." In other words, we fear criticism because it represents failure to us.

When you feel you have failed because of criticism, you have let yourself become *other-directed.* You base your evaluation of your performance on what other people tell you. It's useful to evaluate what other people tell you in an effort to learn from their comments, but their opinion shouldn't define your self-esteem.

The great running back Herschel Walker, who played football at The University of Georgia, was known for his maneuverability and power. Sportscasters often remarked about his "tremendous natural ability." However, when Herschel was a junior in high school and wanted to play football, a kindly coach told him he was too small. The coach advised him to go out for track.

Herschel faced the fear of failure by putting his hands on the outside. He undertook a rigorous training program of calisthenics, running, stretching and careful eating. When he became an All-American football player and Heisman Trophy winner, Herschel said of his success: "My God-given talent is my ability to stick with it longer than anyone else."

When someone criticizes you, don't think you have failed. Just replace the word failure with glitch, hitch, miss, bungle, or false start. Think of a mistake as just another way of doing things. What someone else might call a failure is something from which you intend to learn.

When you put your hands on the outside every day, you're making a commitment to live your life with courage and determination. It symbolizes that you're facing the fears you have about the problems and opportunities the day will bring. George Bernard Shaw said that to be in hell is to drift; to be in heaven is to steer. I challenge you to steer your life with courage and determination as you stand at the open door of opportunity every day. Don't struggle with fear of failure.

You can start practicing the philosophy of putting your hands on the outside tomorrow morning. When you wake up, don't leave your hands on the inside of the covers where it's warm and cozy. Put your hands on the outside – for two reasons: First, you want to maximize your safety when leaving the bed. Second, you want to erase, eradicate and remove any doubt that you're going to stay in that bed a moment longer.

So here is the regimen: Put your hands on the outside, give a giant leap, and choose to make it a great day. When you do that, you won't be limited by the fear of failure as you stand at the open door of opportunity each morning.

Are your hands on the outside?

Conditioning Exercises

Imagine that you're standing at the open door of an airplane getting ready to jump. What do you fear? How can you overcome this fear?

What have you done recently that you called a failure? Can you rename it? For example, can you call it a great learning experience?

Having faced your fear, you're ready to put your hands on the outside and jump successfully into achievement.

When The Winner Awakes

From the time I was five years old, I loved to play the piano. When I was in the eighth grade, I wanted to learn to play Rachmaninoff's *Prelude in C-Sharp Minor.* I wanted to play it perfectly. I wanted an "A" or superior rating at the Spring Music Festival. But I was standing at the open door of opportunity, afraid I wouldn't reach my goal.

Then I decided not to be immobilized by fear. I decided to put my hands on the outside. I went to a store and bought a record of Leonard Pennario, the famous pianist, performing the Rachmaninoff piece. I would put the record on my record player (this was before the days of CDs!), listen to a phrase, pick up the needle, and play the phrase, imitating the nuances I had heard the professional play. Just as paratroopers who put their hands on the outside land safely, I got my superior rating.

You can practice the same mental toughness by tackling things you fear, such as:

- Asking for a raise
- Confronting a teenager's behavior
- Seeking a deeper emotional connection to your spouse or children
- Running for president of your professional association
- Championing your ideas in front of the board of directors
- Writing the novel you've been thinking about for years
- Going back to school for your MBA

Put your hands on the outside and, as Zig Ziglar says, we'll "see you at the top!"

"Go ahead and make mistakes. Make all you can. Because, remember, that's where you'll find success – on the far side of failure."

– Arthur Gordon

"They won't distract you from the wonderful moment of life that you're living right now. They're gone. Let them be gone forever."

DANDELIONS

DAILY MENTAL AEROBIC

Today I will let go of hurt and anger.

"For every minute of anger, you lose 60 seconds of joy."

ANONYMOUS

AS A CHILD, I HAD NO IDEA THAT DANDELIONS WERE WEEDS. I thought they were delightful little flowers that were supposed to dot the lawn in a beautiful yellow pattern.

I loved to pick dandelions and feel their thick blossoms. But I found them even more interesting when they went to seed. The beautiful yellow flowers turned into a hundred little white parachutes. I would take the dandelion that had gone to seed, hold it up and blow. The little parachutes would float away.

That image remains in my mind and helps me to handle the stresses of the day. Every day starts out like a beautiful dandelion, yellow and bright but, typically, goes to seed.

The seeds represent the hurts, disappointments and frustrations of the day. You can rid yourself of daily stresses by pretending that all your anger, hurts and frustrations are little dandelion parachutes. Blow them away each night.

When you do, those negative feelings won't linger into tomorrow's bright sunlight. They won't sap your emotional energy. They won't distract you from the wonderful moment of life that you're living right now. They're gone. Let them be gone forever.

Karla's Coaching Corner

When I read quotes by Aristotle and other ancient philosophers, I'm constantly amazed that they have already stated what I think is a new discovery.

For instance, Aristotle said: "Anybody can become angry – that is easy; but to be angry with the right person and to the right degree and at the right time and for the right purpose and in the right way – that is not within everybody's power and is not easy." In this quote, two fundamental truths can be identified:

1. Everyone feels anger, even if they mask it well.

If you mask anger and don't deal with it appropriately, it will surface in other ways. Trying to mask anger is a little like plugging up a steam vent in a boiler. The steam is stopped in one place, but it will come out somewhere else. If it doesn't, the whole boiler will blow up in your face.

Bottled up emotions are similar. Sooner or later the ghosts of anger rise up to haunt you, usually in damaging ways, and your whole life seems ready to blow up in your face.

2. A little passion applied in the right way at the right time moves events in an appropriate direction.

It's okay to have passion for issues, purposes and causes. This passion can take the form of "appropriate" anger. Your job is to learn what's appropriate. We begin learning this as a children. It doesn't take us long to understand just how far mommy and daddy will let us go with our anger.

Most children learn early that sulking, yelling, breaking things, hitting, or brandishing a plastic Star Wars weapon aren't appropriate expressions of their emotions. When adults still cling to the same childish ways of handling hurt and anger, these behaviors aren't only inappropriate, but invariably move things in extremely negative directions. Anger becomes debilitating and harmful.

So what should you do if anger is a normal emotion to feel, but you can't let it all hang out? Philosopher Thomas Fuller said, "Act nothing in furious passion. It is putting to sea in a storm." To keep yourself out of rough seas where you can't control your ship, try these suggestions:

- ***Change your perception of conflict.***

Conflict is neither right nor wrong. It just is and always will be. There will always be irritations that will cause some anger to rise inside of you. Next time you have a difference of opinion with someone on a sensitive topic, take a position of intrigue. You might say, "Oh, you see it differently? Tell me more. Explain to me why you feel that way. What are your reasons?" Even if you're always "right," when you open your mind you'll find that others also have valid information. As you see their point of view and have the opportunity to express your feelings, your anger will diminish. Who knows – you may end up as allies and you'll be able to let go of anger.

- ***Take direct action when possible.***

The proactive person will take direct action when anger surfaces because of differences of opinion, by doing these kinds of things:

- Making an appointment with the person you're in conflict with
- Turning off the TV and talking with your spouse or child about the conflict
- Researching the topic so you can approach it from a logical, not an emotional, perspective

These are just three suggestions. Be creative. Put your thinking power into deciding what kind of action you can take. As you bring about positive resolutions to conflict, control negative feelings and ready yourself for the next step, you'll find yourself becoming a more powerful person.

- ***Understand what you can and can't control.***

Understanding that there are some things in life over which you don't have control is a huge step toward emotional maturity. Another step is gaining the ability to let go of the situation, just as you would blow away the dandelion seeds. In addition, you can practice acceptance, which is the soulmate of letting go.

Psychologist Ken Dychwald tells the story of meeting Esther Meuller, a head physician in Denmark. Dychwald was in his early 30s and Meuller was 92. He believed that he could learn something from her life's experiences, so he asked her what she had observed about the American people that would help him in his practice.

She said, "You Americans have learned to control so many things to such finite detail that you don't know what to do when you come up against something you can't control, like when a car pulls out in front of you in traffic, or your kid parts his hair on the right side of his head. If you would learn a little more about acceptance, you wouldn't have such high blood pressure."

Thinking about control, I remember an experience I had in 1984. I was driving to a seminar and listening to a newscast about the summer Olympics in Korea. Runner Ben Johnson was accused of using steroids, which he vehemently denied.

To settle the dispute, the manufacturer of the equipment used to detect the steroids was called in to testify. The manufacturer testified that the equipment was so sensitive it could find a teaspoon of sugar in an Olympic-sized pool. I was amazed! Esther Meuller was right. We Americans have become accustomed to an astonishing degree of control.

To safeguard your mental and emotional health, it's important to understand that this type of control isn't possible in all things, especially not in relationships. When you come up against something you can't control, it should take only seconds to recognize that it's uncontrollable. You can then get on with finding a solution or a coping skill that will help you resolve the situation satisfactorily.

Conditioning Exercise

Think about an event that's irritating you. Now decide if the event is controllable or uncontrollable. If it's controllable, take appropriate action to control it.

If the event is uncontrollable, accept the fact, discuss it with someone who is understanding, express your emotions to them, then let go. Find a quiet corner in your house, sit down, and close your eyes.

Visualize in your hand a dandelion that has gone to seed. Feel the hollow stem. See the little parachute seeds. Pretend each seed is an uncontrollable event. Now blow.

Permit your anger, hurt and frustration to float away with the seeds.

You have just taken responsibility for your emotional health. There may be certain events that you can't control, but you can change your emotional response to them by controlling emotions such as anger.

When The Winner Awakes

Life is too short to spend it nursing animosity or keeping a tally of all the wrongs that have come your way. You'll have internalized this mental aerobic if you control your anger, hurt, or frustration when:

- You had a great idea that was implemented and a peer got the credit
- You didn't get the promotion
- Your territory was cut
- Your friend forgot to meet you for a movie
- Your loved one forgot your birthday
- Your child wants you to dissolve or just disappear and doesn't mind telling you

As you take direct action or accept these circumstances, you'll begin to wake up the winner inside.

"Anger, if not restrained, is frequently more hurtful to us than the injury that provokes it."

– Seneca

"I assumed he must not have many problems, because he was climbing the career ladder with lightning speed."

OPPORTUNITY?

DAILY
MENTAL AEROBIC

Today I will use my power of choice.

"If one advances confidently in the direction of his dreams and endeavors to live the life which he has imagined, he will meet with success unexpected in common hours."

HENRY DAVID THOREAU

A FRIEND OF MINE HAD A VERY INFLUENTIAL POSITION IN upper management in a large bank. Whenever I asked him how his job was going, he would say, "Oh, I have a lot of wonderful opportunities."

He said "opportunities" in a humorous way and with a big smile. I looked for hidden messages in his delivery of the word, but couldn't find any. I assumed he must not have many problems, because he was climbing the career ladder with lightning speed.

After I had asked him this question periodically over three years and gotten the same answer, I realized that there was a hidden message. He did have a lot of problems at work, *but he was choosing to see them as opportunities.*

KARLA'S COACHING CORNER

To turn obstacles into opportunities, you need to use three elements:

1. ***Choice***
2. ***Relabeling***
3. ***Humor***

1. The Power of Choice.

My friend was taking responsibility for his own emotional state by exercising his power of choice. He chose to be proactive and take a positive mental perspective.

To understand this phenomenon, think of the letter K. There are two reasons why I use the letter K. First, my name is spelled with a K and I want you to remember that Karla taught you this. Second, it makes a great graphic. The shape of the K shows you how the concept works. The stem of the K represents an event that occurs, something you have labeled as bad. The place where the K splits is the critical point. It's here that you exercise your choice.

You can choose the downward stem and have negative emotions and depression, or you can choose the upward stem, which represents opportunity and growth. When you feel negative emotions, wake up the winner inside by choosing the upward stem of opportunity and growth.

What is the direct application?

If you have a disagreement with your spouse, a child, or a peer at work, you usually label this as a "bad" event and an obstacle to progress.

To reduce the emotional stress of these kinds of events, see the disagreement as an opportunity to clear the air, to talk through differences, and to solve problems before the battle escalates to full-blown war. See your differences as an opportunity to learn. Believe what Charles Colton said: "We owe almost all our knowledge, not to those with whom we have agreed but to those with whom we have differed."

One of the most powerful life lessons I've learned is that the negative and the positive run parallel every day. Both are there for your choosing. By seeing opportunities or obstacles, you cast the deciding vote and become a negative or positive person.

2. The mental skill of relabeling.

The power of choice is closely related to the concept of relabeling. You choose to attach to each event in your life labels such as exciting, dull, terrible, fun, wonderful, and disastrous. The label you choose determines your internal experience.

Words like "terrible" and "disastrous" are closely related to phrases like "huge obstacle" and "big problem." If you stick these labels on everything that happens, you'll be frustrated and will experience distress by the end of the day.

In his book *Kicking Your Stress Habit*, Donald Tubesing says, "If you do not like the distress the label you have attached is causing inside, merely relabel the event." Is this hard? Most definitely. When I read his book, I remember wondering if such a simple skill would really work. Then one day I got a chance to try it out.

I was driving down Lake Lucerne Road near our home and I was angry. I can't remember why, but I was angry. I wanted to get over my anger because my body handles anger with illness and I couldn't afford the time to be sick.

Suddenly, a little voice came to me and said, "Just relabel it." I thought a little longer, then said to myself in a pouty tone of voice, "No! I won't! I want to be angry a bit longer." But it didn't take long for me to start feeling calmer, and then the anger just drifted away.

Let's take another example. You're leaving work and, as you walk out of the building, you see two friends talking. You smile and wave. Both ignore you. You continue on to your car. What are you thinking and feeling?

I'll bet that you were a little embarrassed and that, as your blood pressure started to rise, you were thinking, "Well, they certainly were rude. I just won't invite them to our houseboat party next weekend."

Let's relabel this incident with some alternative thinking. Instead of getting angry, suppose you said these things to yourself:

"They were so involved in their conversation they didn't hear me. It's so hot. I'm glad they didn't hear me. I'd still be there talking. They must have been pretty upset at each other not to even see me. Maybe they're planning a surprise birthday party for me."

In a situation like this, normal humans blame themselves and think of themselves in negative terms. It takes a winner to give others the benefit of a doubt and see several other points of view.

I challenge you to allow the winner inside to relabel every event that causes negative emotions. Even if the only positive label that can be attached is "great learning exercise" or "don't repeat," you'll save yourself years of depression.

3. The magic of humor.

It is reported that a few years ago when Queen Elizabeth was touring the colony of Tonga, someone threw an egg at her as she was getting into the official limousine. It hit her dress. This was extremely embarrassing to all the officials and the good people throughout this hospitable country. Everyone wondered how the Queen would handle this touchy moment when she addressed Parliament the following morning.

With a regal air and queenly courage, she said, "I must admit that I do like an occasional egg, but I much prefer it with my breakfast." At first the laughter was nervous, but it became authentic as everyone realized what she had just done. She had used humor to overcome a bad event. She didn't let the egg incident become an obstacle to the business at hand.

Humor is an effective way for you to handle the negatives of daily living, for a laugh a day keeps the doctor away – literally.

Research on not being so serious began in 1979 when Norman Cousins wrote *Anatomy of an Illness.* Suffering severely from a painful connective tissue disease, Cousins found that ten minutes of belly laughter gave him two pain-free hours and a much improved attitude.

Since Cousin's work, significant research has been carried out in the field of psychoneuroimmunology, which is the study of the communication between the brain (emotions) and the body (immune system).

Controlled studies have revealed that the experience of laughter lowers the level of hormones that harm or deplete the immune system (like cortisol and epinephrine).

At the same time, laughter increases the number and activity of natural killer (NK) cells and T cells. NK cells attack viral or cancerous cells and T cells provide lymphocytes that combat invading toxins. These two types of cells, when not under duress from stress, search and destroy abnormal cells constantly mutating in our bodies.

Long before the age of videos or scientific research, Mark Twain summed up the benefits of laughter when he wrote in *Tom Sawyer*:

"The old man laughed loud and joyfully, shook up the details of his anatomy from head to foot and ended by saying such a laugh was money in a man's pocket because it cut down the doctor's bill like anything."

Conditioning Exercises

Think of a recent event you labeled as bad, an event that's still causing you distress.

Now choose a new label for the event.

Can you find anything humorous in what happened?

By choosing to change the label, you have chosen to be proactive and take control. You have chosen action, which will become energy and motivation.

When The Winner Awakes

You will know you have conquered this mental aerobic when you can find alternative perspectives in situations such as:

Bad Event	Alternative Perspective
The electricity went out before I could finish that report my team leader wants by tomorrow.	Hmm… I think I feel a sick day coming on.
I didn't get the job for which I interviewed.	A better opportunity will come along.
I only had daughters.	My surname will never be tarnished!
The airline lost my golf clubs.	My settlement will buy a much better set.
My e-mail won't work.	Now I remember what it was like in the dark ages!
A vehicle rear-ended me.	Maybe the police officer will be single, like me.
I just finished chemo-therapy.	I'm alive. And I've got a great wig!

Being able to rid yourself of tunnel vision, which restricts you to seeing a situation from only one viewpoint, is one of the most important things you can do for your mental health.

Then, if you add a little humor, who knows what will happen? You may become an optimist!

"I hate doing nothing.
I never know when I'm done."

– Kenny Brandau

"Your brain will believe what you tell it."

AEROBIC ELEVEN **11**

THE WORDS OF WINNERS

DAILY
MENTAL AEROBIC

Today I am a winner. I can do it!

"Winning is a habit.
Unfortunately, so is losing."

VINCE LOMBARDI

I DECIDED I WANTED TO HAVE LOTS OF FUN AND GET LOTS of exercise, so I took up tennis. Lots of fun? I didn't like to lose, so it wasn't much fun. Lots of exercise? Most of the exercise I got was in retrieving my balls from other people's courts. Tennis? Bad choice.

I had joined a neighborhood tennis team and that first team lesson will be etched in my mind forever. It was a balmy spring morning. The instructor, Wally, showed the class how to execute a forehand and I said, "Oh, I can't do that." Then Wally showed us the backhand and I said, "Whoa, I can't do that either."

Next came the serve. Coordinate two hands? I knew I was dead in the water, so I said, "I really can't do this one." Wally stopped the whole class. The park was deathly silent. There was not a bird singing, an airplane going by, or a child playing. Wally said, "Karla, do you realize that you have said, 'I can't' to everything I've tried to teach you this morning?"

I don't say "I can't" any more. I say, "I haven't learned that yet." Or "I'm practicing that one." Or "That's on my to-do list." But never, "I can't." I no longer want to feed my mind with that garbage.

Karla's Coaching Corner

My tennis coach had a powerful emotional impact on me. He helped me to learn that you must have an unshakable, self-renewing belief in your personal power. Saying *I can't* erodes that personal power.

Saying *I can't* puts you in the negative thought mode. Negative thoughts give you negative feelings and prevent you from moving forward mentally and emotionally in your life. The danger of using negative phrases such as *I can't* is that your brain is nondiscriminating.

Your brain will believe what you tell it. If you tell it you're clumsy, what are you? Clumsy. If you tell it you're depressed, what are you? Depressed. If you tell it *I can't,* you may as well not try. You'll never be able to do it.

I can't has a close relative – *I have to.* To understand how devastating that phrase can be, think about the words that might make up the rest of a sentence that begins with *I have to*. It might sound something like this: "I have to, but I don't want to and I wouldn't if I were powerful."

Just as saying *I can't* leaves you feeling powerless, saying *I have to* leaves you feeling like a victim. Both phrases make you work in the hate and fear mode.

Furthermore, *I can't* and *I have to* are false statements. In your heart, you know you can do *anything* you set your mind to, if you're willing to pay the price. Is there anything in the world that you really *have* to do? Do you *have* to go to work? Do you *have* to pay your bills? Do you *have* to send a Mother's Day card?

No! You don't actually have to do any of those things. You can choose not to go to work, choose not to pay the bills, and choose not to send a Mother's Day card. There is a catch, of course. You must accept the consequences for anything you choose <u>not</u> to do. Consequences such as receiving no paycheck, having no money to order pizza, having your electricity turned off, and getting no invitation from Mom to Sunday dinner are no fun.

I can and *I choose* are statements that eliminate negative consequences. *I choose* statements make you powerful. They're a highly overlooked motivational tool, since saying *I choose* is a mature, adult statement that quickly elevates those inner emotions from the hate level to the duty level. You're on your way to the highest productivity level – that of loving what you do.

Coupled with the belief that you can do anything you set your mind to, you'll be unstoppable. When you use the words that constitute the language of achievement, you'll wake up the winner inside and experience self-renewal. You'll walk in the direction of your own choosing and take charge of your own successes. If you want to use the words of winners, try these:

I can. These words symbolize unstoppable belief in your own talents, abilities and personal power.

I will. These words represent your determination to succeed. They dispel the notion that you'll merely "try." You'll accomplish, achieve and triumph over all odds.

I choose to. These words engage your mental abilities to eliminate victim thinking and negative thought patterns.

Conditioning Exercises

Think of something you hate to do, like cleaning the toilet. Close your eyes and visualize yourself doing it. Feel the anger and the hate.

Now say in a loud voice, "I choose to..." and name the thing you hate to do.

Did you feel the magic? Did you feel your emotions change?

Yes? Congratulations! You have just changed yourself from a negative person to a positive person. If you didn't feel the magic, just choose to keep on practicing!

When The Winner Awakes

You'll know you have mastered this aerobic when:

- You start to learn a new software program. It gets frustrating, but you tell yourself, "I can and will do this."
- You begin calling to build a new prospect list and get 27 rejections in a row. You say, "I can and will do this."
- You're asked to enter a competitive dance contest with a friend but you haven't danced for 10 years. You say, "I can and will do this."

If you use this positive self-talk, you may have as interesting an experience as I did several years ago when I joined the tennis team. As members of the Atlanta Lawn and Tennis Association (ALTA), my tennis team competed against another team by playing five matches. To win for the week, our team had to win at least three matches.

One spring morning in April, I was playing in the deciding match. The score was two games each but I was oblivious to this, because I had been missing my high overhead lobs. I was determined to get the next one.

I kept telling myself, "I can do this. I'll get the next one." (For nontennis players, the lob is when the ball is coming to you in an arc, like a rainbow. It's an excellent opportunity for you to smash a winner.) Suddenly, my chance came. My opponent threw up a high lob. I knew I could destroy my opponent this time. It was match point and this was my chance. Not only would I finally demonstrate that I could hit a high lob, I would win the match!

I was so focused on the lob, I was unaware that I was standing right on the baseline. My mind didn't compute the fact that my opponent's shot was going out. If I let it go out, the ball would land outside the baseline and I would win the point.

Instead of leaving the arcing ball to go out, I took a mighty swing at it, giving it all I had. I missed. The ball sailed out. My teammates stood up and cheered. We had won the match because I missed the ball. I decided right there that miracles do happen when you believe in yourself.

"There are only two things you have to do in life. You have to die, and you have to live until you die. You make up all the rest."

– Anonymous

And for those of you who don't like tennis...

"One spring morning, I decided not to ride the Air Dyne. Instead, I jogged around the neighborhood. I learned a valuable lesson."

AEROBIC TWELVE **12**

THE AIR DYNE BICYCLE

DAILY MENTAL AEROBIC

Today I will pursue the intangibles.

"Believe that life is worth living and your belief will help create the fact."

WILLIAM JAMES

BEING OBSESSIVE ABOUT TIME MANAGEMENT, I WANTED TO reduce my exercise time but increase the results. I decided to investigate exercise equipment. As I was looking at exercise bicycles in a local store, the salesman really hooked me. He showed me the Schwinn Air Dyne bicycle, the Cadillac of exercise equipment. At the time, it didn't have any real competition.

The beauty of an Air Dyne is that while you pedal, your hands pump the handle bars, giving your arms and legs a complete workout. The Air Dyne is built on the principle of increasing resistance on a scale from one to ten. At one on the gauge, it's no sweat. At ten, it's a major sweat. Not light sprinkle perspiration, but thunderstorm sweat. And the faster you pedal, the harder it becomes to pedal!

The salesman hooked me with this line: "Madam, on this bicycle, you can get the equivalent of one hour of exercise in only ten minutes." My response was a mixture of disbelief and pure ecstasy. No... surely not... you don't mean that. You do? I'll take ten of them!

What he didn't say was that to get one hour of exercise in ten minutes, you have to ride the Air Dyne between eight and ten on the gauge. My legs could barely pedal at three or four so I learned to cheat. I'll tell you how. I rode for 30 minutes at one on the gauge. It was easy and there was no sweat. That meant no shower, which was a big time saver, and I could still check exercise off my list!

One spring morning, I decided not to ride the Air Dyne. Instead, I jogged around the neighborhood. I learned a valuable lesson: When riding the Air Dyne, you may be efficient, but you can't feel the cool morning air, hear the birds, or experience the invigorating calm of morning.

Karla's Coaching Corner

To me, the cool morning air, the birds' early morning music and the invigorating sense of well-being that comes with a jog in the early hours of the day represent what I call the "intangibles of life."

The "intangibles of life" are the little things that awaken the soul. Being a task-oriented person, this was a hard lesson for me to learn, because I have a difficult time enjoying activities that aren't immediately productive.

I call it the "hate-to-wait syndrome," best explained by an experience I had with my son, Mark. I enrolled him in piano lessons when he was in the first grade. One afternoon when he was practicing, his little hands were zipping right through the half notes, the notes that get two beats. He was treating them like quarter notes that get one beat.

I stopped him and said, "Honey, those are half notes. They get two beats."

"I know," he said. Then through clenched teeth, he continued, "But I hate to wait!" I said to myself, "YES, he is my son!"

When you suffer from the hate-to-wait syndrome, you think time is the enemy. You get impatient and irritable when anyone takes too long to complete a job, to answer a question, or even to finish a sentence. You tend to walk too fast, talk too fast and in general hurry through life in fear that you'll miss some achievement, recognition, or award. Or, horror of all horrors, your productivity will be low and you'll spend an inordinate amount of time on trivia.

My viewpoint changed, however, when I read the transcript of a speech entitled *Time: It's Yours To Use Or Abuse.* The speech was given by William H. Rehnquist, Chief Justice of the United States Supreme Court, at a Boston University Commencement.

I hastily devoured it, eager to see what new insights the Chief Justice could give me about using time more productively. I reasoned that achieving the status of Supreme Court Justice would have taken years of superior self-mastery and excellent time management. I could learn from his experience.

Judge Rehnquist began by stating that the audience doubtless felt they had worked very hard at Boston University to graduate and earn their degree. He continued by saying that this time and effort would be nothing compared to the time demands their chosen occupation would require.

Then he made an insightful statement: "The more successful you are in whatever career you undertake, the greater will be the demands made on your time."

I agreed and thought, "Oh yes! Now tell me how to handle those demands. G ive me new insights into handling the distress they cause. Let the wisdom you have collected over the years come down the ages and train me, a person of a younger generation."

His Honor then quoted Omar Khayam, who said: "The wine of life keeps oozing, drop by drop. The leaves of life keep falling, one by one." The Judge spoke of time as an exhaustible commodity.

"Yes," I agreed again. "I know that. What else, what else? That's not new." I was getting impatient as I continued to read Judge Rehnquist's words.

He said that life's dramas are played out on a number of different stages and you can't do justice to the potential of your own life without sampling not one but several of these various performances.

He stated that it takes time to have a successful career. It takes time to be a good spouse or a good parent, to make new friends but keep the old, to meet the demands of the community, church or political party to which you belong. Also, it takes time to keep your mind fit through hobbies or work in the arts.

Those words went straight to my heart and stirred my

imagination. "Life's dramas are played out on a number of different stages." I nodded. It takes time to be involved in work, family, friends and community.

The performances of my life began to dance before my eyes. I was eager to find out where Judge Rhenquist was going with this.

He continued: "And those of you in the audience who are already rising on the ladders of your chosen careers may murmur that you only wish you had a little time to take advantage of these opportunities.

"Those who are putting in those last few hours at the job tell themselves that they don't have time now, but after they have finally made partner, or finally saved a few more thousand dollars, or gotten a new Mercedes, then at last they will have the time to take advantage of the performances on the other stages of life."

The next part of the speech brought home the Judge's message to me: "Unfortunately, this is a very slippery slope to tread. There are some things that can only be done at a certain time in one's life. You can only be a parent to a child while the child is young." Ah yes, this was the message. There are many dramas that are part of the human experience, but you can't enact them all at once. It's okay to sequence life's performances.

In my mind, I saw a huge auditorium that contained four stages, each with open curtains and a drama performance in progress. I was performing in all four dramas! I would say my lines in one production, then slip through the curtains and enter a scene on another stage.

I chuckled at the thought of my doomed attempt to juggle the stages of life and decided that I needed to shut down "My Community," and let "All My Children" play instead. There were many applications running through my mind, but the one that was my greatest flash of inspiration was this: While I'm performing on one stage, what's happening on another stage may seem trivial, but may later prove to be important.

For instance, just as you can only be a parent to children when they're young, you can only do things in other relationships when the need arises. You don't cement friendships when you call and say, "Patti, you remember you called me about six months ago. What was it you needed?"

Since junior high school, I've had a "to-do" list branded on my forehead. I've known that, to be an achiever, I had to be efficient and effective, as I thought I would be on the Air Dyne bicycle.

But after letting the wisdom of the Chief Justice of the Supreme Court of the United States of America touch me, I decided it was time to experience a little more of the trivial. I decided to take time for the "trivial intangibles" that awaken the soul, such as jogging in the neighborhood in the cool of the morning.

I now have a new item to check off every day. Ma Bell spent an entire decade saying, "Reach out and touch someone." We should heed that advice, be it family or friend!

So swing in your hammock, plant flowers at your front door, or pet your cat, and you'll experience the intangibles of life that awaken the soul.

Conditioning Exercises

Contemplate your life.

Are you missing the intangibles that awaken the soul?

On which stages of life are you performing now?
Are they command performances?

Do you have a stage where the
dramas have not started?

When will you begin writing your script?

When The Winner Awakes

You'll know that you understand this mental aerobic when you can make a variation of the Pareto Principle work for you. I call this variation the 20/20 rule, but let's start with the Pareto Principle.

The Pareto Principle states that 80% of the activities consuming a normal day don't bring the desired results. It's the remaining 20% that contains the greatest rewards and moves individuals toward their goals. This means that you must concentrate on, and be highly effective with, at least 20% of your daily activities to stay on top of your job and to contribute to your company's success. Does this mean that the remaining 80% of your activities are a total waste of time? Definitely not. Legitimate tasks consume 30% of the remaining 80%. These legitimate tasks include returning phone calls, writing correspondence and responding to the needs of your peers.

Great care should be taken with the next 30% of your time, however. This is typically taken up with frenetic activities that should be questioned for their validity and carefully scrutinized for the timewasters that can be deeply embedded in them.

The remaining 20% represents intangibles, traditionally called "going the extra mile" or "giving it the personal touch." For instance, a young lady came into my office, slumped down in my chair and, with tearful eyes, said, "Karla, I need a hug. I don't feel like I'm worth anything today." Those are the times to take off the watch, cover the clock and forget about efficiency. Intangibles aren't always urgent, but they're always vital.

Winners follow the 20/20 rule instead of the 80/20 rule: They spend at least 20% of the day on high-priority work and 20% of the day on vital intangibles. They do this because the 20/20 rule will not only increase the bottom line, it will improve your inner peace and happiness too.

"You can do anything you want to do, but you can't do everything."

– Karla Brandau

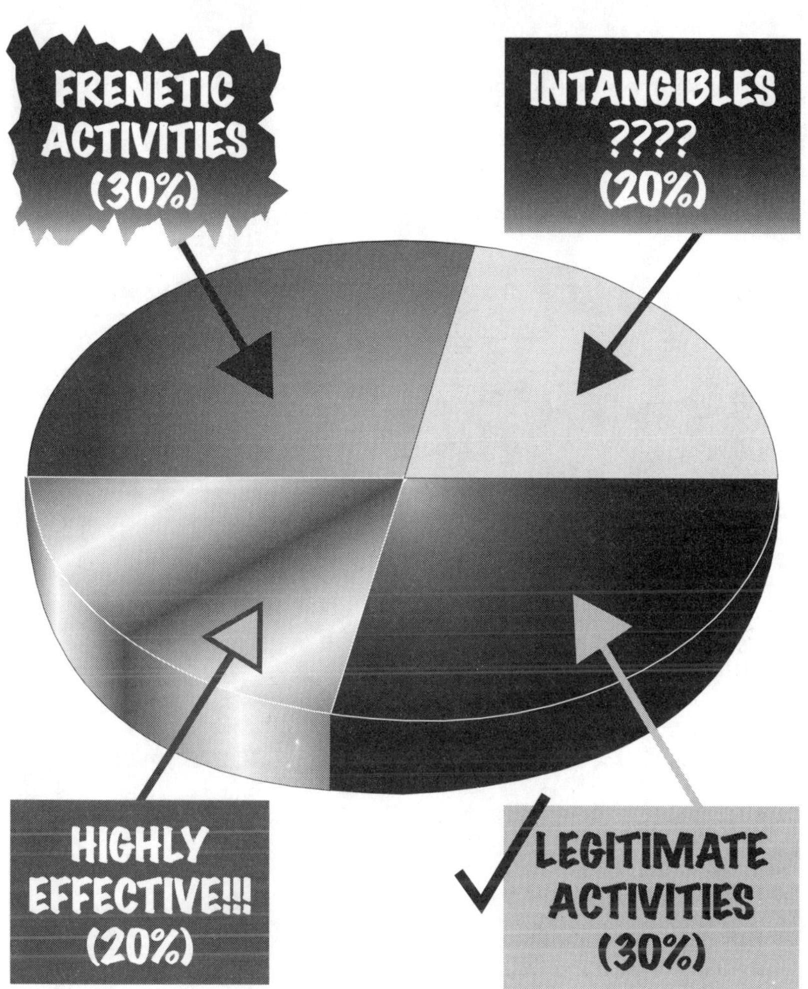

LEGITIMATE + FRENETIC = 60%

HIGHLY EFFECTIVE + INTANGIBLES = 40% = THE 20/20 RULE

"I can't walk down any beach now without Steve's words ringing in my ears."

AEROBIC THIRTEEN

13

SEA DEBRIS OR BLUE SKIES?

DAILY
MENTAL AEROBIC

Today I will look up.

"In solitude we give passionate attention to our lives, to our memories, to the details around us."

VIRGINIA WOOLF, FROM
A ROOM OF ONE'S OWN

LAST YEAR MY HUSBAND STEVE AND I DID SOMETHING different for Christmas. We left Atlanta and went to St. George Island off the Gulf Coast of Florida. We wanted to get away from the normal frenetic pace of life and celebrate in a quiet, gentle way.

One morning, just before dawn, we were walking down the beach. Looking down, I saw broken shells, dirty army-green foam, a piece or two of plastic and an abandoned Styrofoam ball. Farther down the beach were a telephone pole and a tree trunk with roots still attached.

Seeing this pollution, several questions entered my mind: "How did the tree get there? Why can't I find perfect sea shells like the gift shops have? Why do people litter? What in the world do the birds find to eat in the sand?"

As I was lost in these thoughts, my husband said, "Don't look down. Look up!" I looked up. The beauty made me speechless. The sun was breaking through the clouds, turning them from dark and foreboding to white, puffy and playful. The shades of pink, red and orange were spectacular, especially against the brilliant blue. The water turned to a blue green. The miracle of dawn was occurring.

I can't walk down any beach now without Steve's words ringing in my ears: "Look UP!" As you walk through your existence, don't look down at what litters your life. Look up and you'll find unspeakable beauty.

Karla's Coaching Corner

This experience had three lessons for me:

1. ***Have faith and hope***
2. ***Be an optimist***
3. ***Renew your body and soul***

1. Have faith and hope.

To me, the simple phrase my husband used was powerful: Look up. It symbolized the faith I have in God and the positive feelings that can come from the belief that there's a force – a higher power – outside of myself who can help me through tough times in my life. But faith shouldn't be invested in the Supreme Being alone. There must also be faith in the process of life.

Sales professionals wouldn't get on the phone and make calls if they didn't have faith that the calls would result in closed sales. You would never start a diet and begin an exercise program if you didn't have faith that you would lose weight, trim up and increase your energy.

Faith and belief in the process, combined with faith and belief in a power outside of yourself, can bring you exceptional levels of hope. Faith and hope work together to help you make resolves, apply yourself in achieving your goals, and use persistence no matter how tough the going gets.

This is particularly important when you're two hours into your diet, the scales have not moved an ounce, and you're reaching ravenously for the refrigerator door!

2. Be an optimist.

It's normal human behavior to be a pessimist. In fact, researchers say that 70% of our thoughts are negative. When I heard that statistic, it made me realize what a superhuman effort it takes to be a positive person, to look up at the blue sky instead of down at life's debris.

Looking down at the debris is similar to having a goal, running into a roadblock and stopping dead. Most humans lack the ability to concentrate on the end result and "play through" the obstacle, to use a sports term. "Playing through" means that you don't stop for minor aches and pains.

Just as I noted every imperfect thing about the beach, potential losers add to their "negativity reservoir" by noticing and counting every flaw in their surroundings.

They become so bogged down with judgments that they have great difficulty letting themselves experience pleasure.

Potential losers weigh themselves down with what I call "emotional rocks." They carry around unresolved problems and conflicts. They sprinkle their chitchat liberally with present hardships and rehash tragedies from the past. The emotional rocks they carry literally sink their ambitions and desires by immobilizing them with what seem like insurmountable problems.

This is much like a story told by Mark O. Haroldsen in his book *Goals, Guts and Greatness*. He tells of being invited to go fishing with his neighbors. The father told him to be ready at 5:00 AM. Mark was so excited, that he couldn't sleep and consequently he didn't fall asleep until 3:00 AM, which caused him to sleep through his alarm.

At 5:30 AM, he awoke with terror in his heart. He pulled on his clothes, ran outside and, sure enough, he had been left behind. He thought he could find them so he jumped on his bike, rode through the town and up the canyon.

He searched in vain for two hours with great energy. When he couldn't find them and turned his bike to go home, he explains: "All my energy was gone. It seemed to take forever to get back home, even though it was mostly downhill. Every bump seemed to be an insult. Every slight hill seemed to be a mountain. I moped around the house the rest of the day, spending much of the time in bed because I didn't have the energy to do anything else."

When I read this, I thought of many times in my life when I had experienced a disappointment and spent the rest of the day, week or month immobilized.

Your positive thoughts and expectations create energy in you. Negative thoughts steal energy and literally sink your dreams. Instead, learn to focus on your dreams and your goals when you hit roadblocks. If you do, motivation and ambition will soon replace despair.

3. Renew your body and soul.

Hans Selye, one of the first researchers into stress, made an interesting statement: "There are two main types of human beings: 'racehorses' who thrive on stress and are only happy with a vigorous, fast-paced lifestyle, and 'turtles' who, in order to be happy, require peace, quiet and a generally tranquil environment."

I believe that successful individuals are able to switch between one mentality and the other. They understand when to be a turtle and when to be a racehorse. For instance, they know that when project deadlines have to be met, or new sales products are being rolled out, the racehorse mentality will bring tasks to completion on time. Racehorses scramble, hustle, remain conscious of time and complete the plan. Statements such as "the early bird gets the worm" and "time is money" reinforce the racehorse part of your soul.

But what if your natural style is turtle behavior? In that case, you need to learn to be a racehorse only when it's appropriate. Conversely, if your natural style is racehorse behavior, you'll have to learn turtle behavior in order to replenish inner reserves. Downtime is critical.

Walking the beach and looking up is turtle behavior. It lets you unwind and replenishes your inner strength. It helps you overcome the fragmentation that happens with a fast-paced lifestyle. It opens your mind to new and creative ideas. Life ceases to be superficial and takes on a deeper meaning. Walking the beach each day and getting in touch with your inner self is just as important as a nutritious diet and a good night's sleep. But turtle behavior need not be confined to leisure time.

Typical turtle activities in the workplace are long-range planning, strategic thinking and mediating so that people's opinions become synthesized. In work situations, the job of the turtle is to bring the racehorses together and make sure they run as a cohesive team.

Conditioning Exercises

Make turtle behavior a habit.

If you don't live at the ocean and a beach is not available, take a walk in a park or install a hammock under your trees. If you can't find a quiet place, visit a beach in your thoughts. Let the peace you experience be a reservoir of inner strength.

Do it every day.

Pick a certain hour of the day when you will meditate, or "walk on the beach and look up." It will calm your mind and renew your inner self. Where will this be? What time of day will this be?

Give yourself permission to exhibit turtle behavior for 21 days straight.

As turtle behavior becomes a habit, you'll be in touch with an inner self you have not talked to since childhood.

Remember the days when you sat watching the sand flow through your fingers or rode your bike down little hills and through streets lined with big trees? Your mind was free to be calm and you were infused with a new enthusiasm for life. Learn to look up and give thanks. You'll experience this calmness once more.

When The Winner Awakes

You'll know that this aerobic means something to you when you can delight in the beauty of the natural wonders around you, take time to enjoy the flower that has just burst into bloom, or savor the sweet smell of the air after a rainstorm.

In these moments, you put aside the value of your stock, the backstabbing to become chairman of the board, or the anxiety of raising money for your high school's new football stadium.

This aerobic will have positively impacted your life when you have the faith to do these kinds of things:

- Apply for a management position in your organization
- Start your own business
- Write a book
- Seek a patent on a new process you invented

- Run for office in your professional association
- Start investing in real estate
- Take up golf, tennis or some other sport
- Volunteer to coach your child's little league team

You'll know that you understand this aerobic if you can separate racehorse from turtle behavior. Use racehorse behavior when you are:

- Doing repetitive tasks
- Working through a routine workload
- Handling the trivia of life

Use turtle behavior when you are:

- Relating to people
- Concentrating on a major presentation
- Seeking to influence decisions

This aerobic will make you a winner when you handle disappointments with optimism for a better day. Here's an example. My daughter, Susan, is a star athlete. If she was depressed after a loss, her favorite coach, Hugh Buchanan, would tell her, "Aw, Susan, the sun will still come up tomorrow." She always felt better.

You'll also feel better if you internalize the belief in tomorrow that "looking up" can give you. You'll be optimistic, like little Annie in the Broadway musical. She always believed her dreams would come true tomorrow and they did!

The winner inside you will awake as you use faith, hope, optimism and self-renewal to build inner reservoirs of personal power and strength. You'll be able to look up at the blue skies of life and not down at the debris that litters your world.

"Look up to success!
Expect success to happen and in a strange, magical, mystical way, it will."

– Karla Brandau

"To improve, you must make
your weaknesses your strengths."

– Pat Summitt,
University of Tennessee
women's basketball coach and
winner of two national championships

"Ability is what you're capable of doing.
Motivation determines what you do.
Attitude is how well you do it."

– Lou Holtz,
Former football coach at
the University of Notre Dame

THE COOL DOWN

Don't I Know You From Somewhere?

Although I'm neither telepathic nor psychic, I feel that I know you simply because you have read this book. You have shared my thoughts about life. My greatest desire is that, as you read these pages, you found a personal power unequaled in your previous experience.

If you follow the principles described in this book, the winner inside you will wake up, and that winner will make a difference in the world. The winner inside will infuse the people you touch with something that can't be duplicated – a love of life.

The winner inside will find that success does not sneak in through a back door, but enters confidently through the front entrance, head held high.

If the winner inside you has awoken, please share your experience with me. You can contact me through:

Life Power Dynamics
P. O. Box 450802
Atlanta, GA 31145-0802
Tel: 770-923-0883
Fax: 770-931-2530
E-mail: karla@kbrandau.com
Web site: www.kbrandau.com

About The Author

Karla Brandau is President of Life Power Dynamics, a company she founded in 1986 to assist corporations and their employees to increase profits through improved leadership, interpersonal relationships and personal competence. Her clients include Coca-Cola, Chick-fil-A, Crawford & Company, Safeco, Motorola, United States Environmental Protection Agency, Digital Equipment Corporation and Lucent Technologies.

Karla graduated cum laude from Brigham Young University, has been an instructor for the American Management Association, and is a past president of Georgia Speakers Association. She is currently serving on the Chapter Leadership Board for National Speakers Association. She is a member of the Business and Technology Alliance, the American Society for Training and Development, Meeting Professionals International, and she is listed in *Who's Who of Executive Women.*

Her latest book, *Wake Up the Winner Inside,* is designed to help individuals handle the increased mental and emotional pressures associated with downsizing, reengineering and the laser speed of life in the technological age. Her tape series, entitled *Time For Results,* accelerates personal success by helping people to get the results they want out of life.

Karla has been featured on television and radio shows. She has written articles for periodicals such as *The Georgia Printer* and *Optometry News.* She is a volunteer for many school and community activities, including the Boy Scouts of America and the Georgia Tech women's basketball team.

On the personal side, Karla has been married for 30 years and has three children. She has interviewed Gladys Knight, occasionally makes 4-5 letter words in Scrabble, has an irrepressible sense of humor, and prefers her strawberries dipped in milk chocolate.

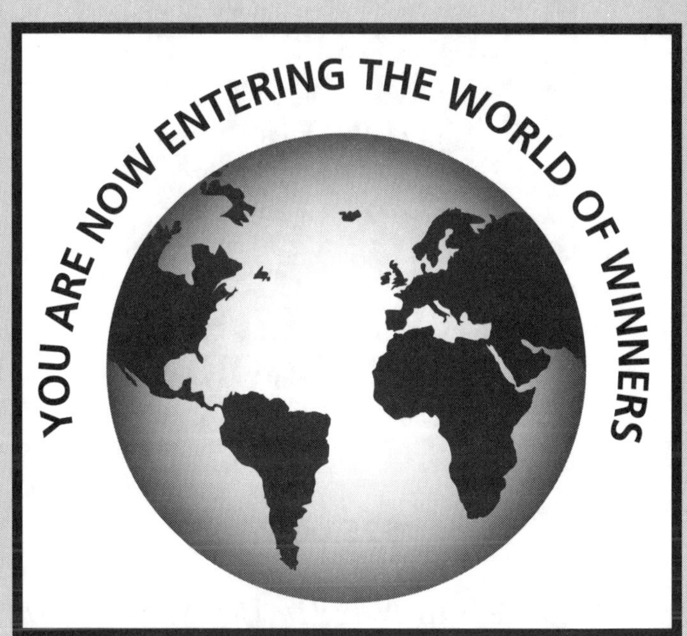

KARLA'S LEARNING TOOLS

Workbook

$25.00

This companion to *Wake Up The Winner Inside* is a personal workbook you can use to make your future unfold. It contains space to record your thoughts as you internalize each aerobic and think through each conditioning exercise. In addition, you can record your mental and emotional progress toward the mindset of a winner. The greatest benefit of the workbook, however, is the journal space it provides. This journal space will remind you to look for "Blue Skies" every day, not "Sea Debris." You can then record each occasion you looked up to see significant and wonderful events happening to you.

This Winner's Workbook will becomes your "joy journal" on your journey to success. Accelerate your personal success by ordering it today.

Workbook

$25.00

At last – a goal setting workbook that doesn't superficially tell you about goals. Invent Your Future shows you a step-by-step process to articulate your needs, translate them into goals, then write an action plan to put you in control of your life.

As you learn how to write your personal vision and mission statements, expect a transformation in your personal power. This systematic process will show you the values that are most central to your life and give you tips on how to live your life by your values. The workbook will prompt you to design the "big picture" of your life. It will also teach you to sort and sequence your life's goals and objectives, as you make strategic plans for personal and professional growth. Furthermore, you'll learn how to remove blocks to goal achievement.

Buy this workbook and take full responsibility for your life. You will enter an elite echelon of achievers.

Quote Books

These delightful books, which are filled with inspiring quotes from a host of successful people, serve as perfect companion pieces to *Wake Up The Winner Inside.*

Dance With The Sunbeams of Life

$10.00

Quotes to make you smile, laugh and lighten your day.

Empowering Thoughts

$10.00

Quotes to stretch your mind and spirit
and inspire you to greater heights of achievement.

Book

Reach For The Stars

$19.00

This compelling anthology of success by 20 nationally known speakers will lift your spirits and motivate you to take action. *Reach For The Stars* contains a galaxy of ideas that will help you to strengthen relationships, move up, make money and drop stress.

This wonderfully entertaining book features Karla's invaluable work on *The Compelling Persona,* a guide based on her observations of the characteristics possessed by compelling individuals. It will show you how to develop more purpose, integrity, charisma and collaboration skills.

Audio Tape Series

Time For Results
$15.00

Get $25,000 ideas to give you the ultimate results when you invest your time in any activity.

This hard-hitting audio series is a must for anyone who is results-oriented. It will show you how to do what you value, prioritize conflicting demands, and find time for the things you really want to do.

You'll learn how to perform in "The Zone," where work is play, problem-solving abilities are on the edge, and the right amount of urgency is created for innovation. Take time out, take *Time For Results.*

Video Program

No More Excuses!
Become a Person of Influence

$20.00

The Magnetic Personality shows you how to develop a charismatic and engaging persona. Karla will teach you how to assess your personal power and develop traits that will take you to the next level of achievement. In addition, you'll learn how to connect with people who have a different style from you.

From this enlightening video, you'll learn about yourself and how people perceive you. Your increased self-knowledge will improve all your relationships, including those with your spouse and your children.

Karla's invaluable tips and ideas will help you to structure a long-term self-improvement program that will bring about unprecedented changes in behavior.

PERSONALITY ASSESSMENT

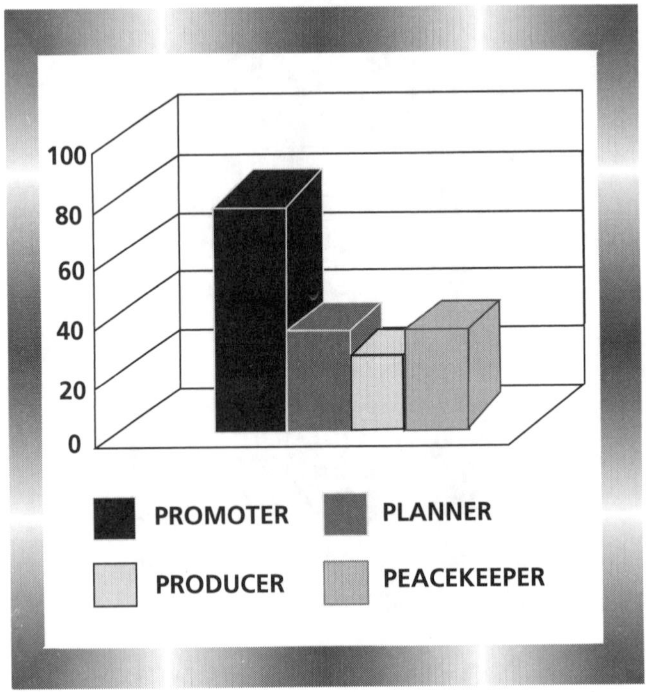

THE HUMAN BEHAVIOR DEPUZZLER

$15.00

This unique assessment system comes in the form of a questionnaire. It's a simple indicator that will show you how people perceive you and how you project yourself. It was created by Vicki Barnes, a certified typologist and president of Vicki Barnes Seminars, who teaches at the University of California at Irvine. It was validated by Dr. James Schmook, who teaches at Stanford University. Dr. Schmook has a doctorate in leadership and learning.

When you send in the questionnaire, you will get back a detailed assessment, plus a bar graph showing your personality mix. Take advantage of this invaluable opportunity to see yourself as others see you, so that you can make whatever changes to your behavior you want.

Karla's Professional Services

STRATEGIC SUCCESS UNIVERSITY

A Value-Based Performance System to Accelerate Success

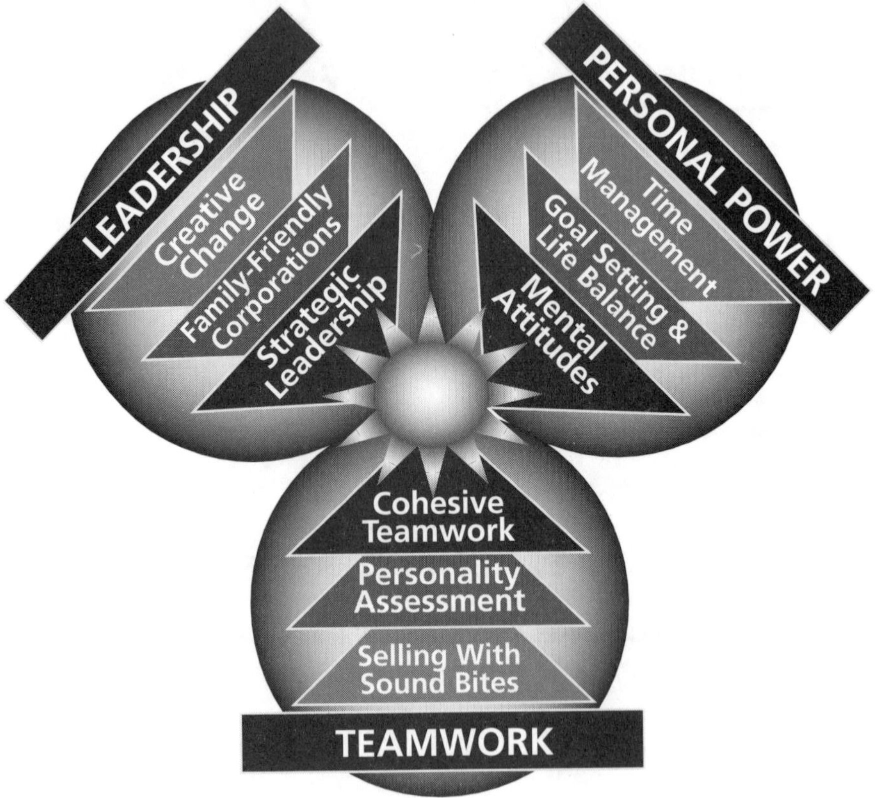

Bring these principles to your organization and make the people and profit connection

Modules in this outstanding success system can be taught over one intensive week, delivered at a full weekend retreat, or customized for a revolutionary 12-month training program.

KARLA BRANDAU: Leadership Coach, Teamwork Specialist, Empowerment Mentor

Keynotes, Workshops, and Breakout Sessions

Imagine what would happen if you could WAKE UP THE WINNER inside every person in your organization! They would come to work each morning with a winner's attitude. Innovation and productivity would go sky high, while problems would be met with a quiet determination to succeed.

Bring this power to your organization with Karla's system for acquiring new habits and work relationships that will WAKE UP THE WINNERS in your organization and improve profits.

Karla's powerful leadership and team building concepts are delivered as keynotes, workshops, or breakout sessions. See next page for program titles and topics covered.

Highlights of Programs With Principles Guaranteed to Transform Your Work Environment

WAKE UP THE WINNER INSIDE
• Mental Attitudes

A WHAP AND A ZAP TO THE BRAIN
• Creative Change

HARMONIZE YOUR LIFE
• Goal Setting and Life Balance

WORKING FOR THE SOARING DESIGN RESEARCH CENTER
• Strategic Leadership

SEE OTHERS WITH 20/20 VISION
• Personality Assessment

HOW TO MAKE IT IN THE CORPORATE BIG LEAGUES
•Teamwork

All modules can be customized for executives, managers, support staff and teams.

How To Order Karla's Learning Tools and Contract For Her Services

To order Karla's books, audio tapes and videos, please go to her Website: http://www.kbrandau.com. There, you can download an order form to be mailed in or faxed, or order on line by credit card through a secure server.

To obtain further details of Karla's professional services, or to engage her for a keynote, workshop, breakout session, or full training program, contact her at the following address:

Life Power Dynamics
P. O. Box 450802
Atlanta, GA 31145-0802
Tel: 770-923-0883
Fax: 770-931-2530
E-mail: karla@kbrandau.com
Web site: http://www.kbrandau.com

Karla's Suggested Reading List

My winning attitude has been influenced tremendously by people who have shared their ideas through their writing. This is my suggested reading list. It will assist you in the daily process of maintaining mental and emotional health. The wisdom found in these books will help you stabilize your emotions, dump emotional baggage and cement a winner's attitude.

Enjoy!

As A Man Thinketh by James Allen. Bookcraft.

The Things That Matter Most by Lowell L. Bennion. Publishers Press.

10 Seeds of Greatness by Denis Waitley. Fleming H. Revell Company.

Real Magic by Wayne W. Dyer. Harper Collins Publishers.

Overcoming Hurts & Anger by Dwight L. Carlson, M.D. Harvest House Publishers.

Nobody's Perfect by Dr. Hendrie Weisinger & Norman M. Lobsenz. Warner Books.

Caring Enough To Confront by David Augsburger. Herald Press.

Go For It! by Dr. Irene C. Kassorla. Dell Publishing.

Psycho-cybernetics by Maxwell Maltz. Wilshire Book Company.

What To Say When You Talk To Your Self by Shad Helmstetter, Ph.D. Pocket Books.

Learned Optimism by Martin E. P. Seligman, Ph.D. Alfred A. Knopf, Inc.

Your Erroneous Zones by Dr. Wayne W. Dyer. Avon.

The Psychology Of Self-Esteem by Nathaniel Branden. Bantam Books.

The 7 Habits of Highly Effective People by Stephen R. Covey. Simon & Schuster.

Release Your Brakes by James W. Newman. Warner Books.

Living A Beautiful Life by Alexandra Stoddard. Random House.

Stress Without Distress by Hans Seyle. Harper & Row Publishers, Inc.

The Magic Of Conflict by Thomas F. Crum. Simon & Schuster.

The Encouragement Book by Don Dinkermeyer & Lewis E.Losoney. Prentice Hall Press.

The Now Habit by Neil Fiore, Ph.D. Tarcher.

Perfectionism – What's Bad About Being Too Good? by Miriam Adderholdt-Elliott, Ph.D. Free Spirit Publishing.

Man's Search For Meaning by Victor E. Frank. Simon & Schuster.

Control Theory – A New Explanation Of How We Control Our Lives by William Glasser, M.D. Harper & Row, Publishers.

Kicking Your Stress Habits by Donald A. Tubesing, Ph.D. Signet.

Stress by Walter McQuade and Ann Aikman. E.P. Dutton & Company.

The Road Less Traveled by M. Scott Peck, M.D. Simon & Schuster.